Church

Enjoying God's masterpiece

by Anne Woodcock

Church: Enjoying God's masterpiece
The Good Book Guide to the church
© The Good Book Company, 2021
Series Consultants: Tim Chester, Tim Thornborough,
                    Anne Woodcock, Carl Laferton

Published by:
The Good Book Company

thegoodbook.com | thegoodbook.co.uk
thegoodbook.com.au | thegoodbook.co.nz | thegoodbook.co.in

ISBN: 9781784984199

Printed in Turkey

CONTENTS

Introduction: Good Book Guides

Every Bible-study group is different—yours may take place in a church building, in a home or in a cafe, on a train, over a leisurely mid-morning coffee or squashed into a 30-minute lunch break. Your group may include new Christians, mature Christians, non-Christians, moms and tots, students, businessmen or teens. That's why we've designed these *Good Book Guides* to be flexible for use in many different situations.

Our aim in each session is to uncover the meaning of a passage, and see how it fits into the "big picture" of the Bible. But that can never be the end. We also need to appropriately apply what we have discovered to our lives. Let's take a look at what is included:

⊕ **Talkabout:** Most groups need to "break the ice" at the beginning of a session, and here's the question that will do that. It's designed to get people talking around a subject that will be covered in the course of the Bible study.

⊕ **Investigate:** The Bible text for each session is broken up into manageable chunks, with questions that aim to help you understand what the passage is about. The **Leader's Guide** contains **guidance for questions**, and sometimes ⊗ additional "follow-up" questions.

⊡ **Explore more (optional):** These questions will help you connect what you have learned to other parts of the Bible, so you can begin to fit it all together like a jig-saw; or occasionally look at a part of the passage that's not dealt with in detail in the main study.

→ **Apply:** As you go through a Bible study, you'll keep coming across **apply** sections. These are questions to get the group discussing what the Bible teaching means in practice for you and your church. ⊡ **Getting personal** is an opportunity for you to think, plan and pray about the changes that you personally may need to make as a result of what you have learned.

↑ **Pray:** We want to encourage prayer that is rooted in God's word—in line with his concerns, purposes and promises. So each session ends with an opportunity to review the truths and challenges highlighted by the Bible study, and turn them into prayers of request and thanksgiving.

The **Leader's Guide** and introduction provide historical background information, explanations of the Bible texts for each session, ideas for **optional extra** activities, and guidance on how best to help people uncover the truths of God's word.

Why study the church?

If you have never before investigated what the Bible tells us about the church of Jesus Christ, you are, I hope, in for a wonderful surprise. Few things present a more astonishing contrast than the way most people view church today and what the Bible tells us about the church. Even some who have followed Christ for years might be missing out on the whole breathtaking truth about the gathered people of God that we find in the pages of Scripture.

There are various reasons why this might be. Throughout church history, there have always been groups professing to follow Christ but who then stray from the central truths of Scripture. With Bible teaching illuminating our minds on this subject, we start to see that some organisations identifying as churches are anything but.

Then, of course, every church is peopled by sinners—those saved by Jesus, yes, but all still struggling with weakness and temptation, and who sometimes fail badly. So churches can at times be painful places, even for faithful and mature Christians. At other times church can just feel like a slog: a lot of hard work with very little reward. We might therefore be tempted to let our difficult experiences of church blind us to the promise of Jesus Christ: "I will build my church, and the gates of Hades will not overcome it" (Matthew 16:18).

If disappointment or difficulty with church affect you, or if you're simply unsure of what the Bible says about church, here's an opportunity to unearth these unimaginably wonderful truths about the people with whom you gather week by week. As you investigate seven key characteristics of the church of Christ set out in the New Testament, you'll learn what God is doing in and through you together.

My prayer is that you will come to see your particular Christian fellowship—though weak, prone to error and unimpressive in worldly terms—as nothing less than part of the ultimate masterpiece of our loving heavenly Father. With that renewed understanding, you can grow in your enjoyment of what God, through his Son's sacrifice of atonement and the power of the Spirit, is crafting in his church.

1

GOD'S PEOPLE

⊕ talkabout

1. What comes to mind when you hear the word "church"?

In the Bible, the word "church" is used in two ways that overlap.

- All believers everywhere throughout history. We join the church in this sense when we are born again by the Holy Spirit and become a follower of Jesus. This total church cannot be seen now but will be revealed in the new creation.

- A local group of believers. We join the church in this sense when, having become a follower of Jesus, we commit ourselves to the community and activities of a local Christian gathering, and put ourselves under the teaching and pastoral care of the leaders there.

⊕ investigate: all believers everywhere

❯ Read 1 Peter 1:1-2

It's evident from this greeting that Peter was writing to multiple churches in what is now modern-day Turkey—although his words here also apply to Christian readers throughout time (there are similarities with other New Testament letter greetings, such as 1 Corinthians 1:2; 2 Corinthians 1:1; and James 1:1).

2. How does Peter describe the people he is writing to?

> **DICTIONARY**
>
> **Apostle (v 1):** one of a group of men chosen by Jesus to be the first leaders of the church (all his followers in all places).
> **Elect (v 1):** people chosen by God and saved by him from their sin.
> **Sanctifying (v 2):** making holy.
> **Sprinkled with [Jesus'] blood (v 2):** cleansed from sin by Jesus' death.

• What's comforting and what's challenging about his description?

3. How does Peter's description contrast with commonly-held views in our culture today of what a church is?

> ❯ **Read 1 Peter 2:9-10**

Having contrasted those who reject Jesus Christ with those who trust in him (2:1-8), Peter launches into another description of all the followers of Jesus.

4. Peter previously described the followers of Jesus as "scattered". Here, how are we united? (Think about our identity and our role.)

5. Peter previously described the followers of Jesus as "exiles"—those who are homeless and seen as outsiders. Here, what shows our privileged status?

6. What do we learn here about...

• our relationship with God?

• our mission in this world?

• the contrast between our past and our present?

⊡ **explore more**

optional

God has always aimed to create a people that he calls his own. David wrote this song celebrating God's proactive love for his Old Testament people, Israel.

▶ **Read Psalm 68:1-10, 32-35**

As you answer the questions, note the similarity of relationship between God and his people in Psalm 68, and God and the church in 1 Peter.

Verses 1-3 sets out two groups. How are God's enemies described?

What marks out his people here?

In verses 4-6, what do we learn about God? What do we learn about his people?

From verses 7-10, list the things that God has done in history for his people. What have his people done?

In verses 32-35 David lists reasons to give God praise and glory. What do God's people contribute?

→ apply

7. As scattered exiles, the church is weak and out of place in society, and often without rights. But as God's chosen people and special possession, the church is also the astoundingly privileged royalty of the universe. What practical difference should both truths make in our attitude towards Christ's church?

⊡ getting personal

"Brothers and sisters, think of what you were when you were called. Not many of you were wise ... influential ... of noble birth. But God chose the foolish things of the world ... the weak things ... the lowly things ... and the despised things ... so that no one may boast before him." (1 Corinthians 1:26-29)

Christians look weak and lowly in the eyes of the world. Are you able to accept that joyfully—or do you instinctively feel resistant to the idea? How does it help to remember that this displays God's power and wisdom, not ours?

⊙ investigate: the first local church

❯ Read Acts 2:42-47

The word "church" is not mentioned in Acts until chapter 5, but as the Greek word itself simply means "gathering", there can be no doubt that here Luke is describing the first church ("together" appears three times).

DICTIONARY

Breaking of bread (v 42): eating together (Luke 24:30-31, 35); or celebrating the Lord's Supper together (Luke 22:19-20); or both (1 Corinthians 11:20-27).

8. What essential features of a local church are listed here?

9. How would this description of a church surprise people in your culture today, do you think?

⊇ **apply**

10. Read through the features of the first church again. In what ways is your church like this one?

• In what ways is it different? Why, do you think?

11. How could you help your church to be as much like the first Jerusalem church as possible?

⊕ pray

Thank God that you and your church are part of his chosen people, his royal priesthood, his holy nation and his special possession.

Ask for his help to live in obedience to Jesus while you are scattered exiles in this world.

Pray for your church to become more and more like the first church, and for yourself to be more and more like those brothers and sisters in Jerusalem.

2 Revelation 5:1-14; Matthew 28:18-20
GOD'S KINGDOM

⊕ talkabout

1. What king (or queen) fascinates you and why? (Think past or present, real or fictional!)

• Would you want to be a citizen of their kingdom? Why or why not?

⊕ investigate

❯ Read Revelation 5:1-14

In a vision the apostle John witnesses the church as seen in God's throne room in heaven—and therefore as it truly is. The song (v 9-10) explains what John sees and hears in the vision of the Lamb, who alone is able to open the scroll (v 1-7) and bring about God's kingdom (v 10).

2. Who and what is this part of John's vision about? (See especially v 6, 9-10.)

> **DICTIONARY**
>
> **Scroll (v 1):** God's plan of salvation. Opening the seals signifies the ability to implement this.
> **The Lion / Root (v 5):** descriptions of the Rescuer-King, promised by God to his people (see Genesis 49:8-10; Isaiah 11:1-10).
> **Lamb (v 6):** Jesus, "the Lamb of God" (John 1:29).
> **The four living creatures (v 6):** representing the whole of creation.
> **The 24 elders (v 6, 8):** representing the church; all God's people throughout history.

3. What do we learn here about God's kingdom?

• Its people (v 9-10)

• Its purpose (v 9-10)

• Its King (v 11-14)

optional

🎲 explore more

700 years before Jesus, the Old Testament prophet Isaiah looked forward to the time when God's King and his kingdom would be revealed. This passage is famous as one of the best-known prophecies about Jesus.

▶ **Read Isaiah 9:2-7**

What does this prophecy tell us about the goodness of the rule of the King of God's kingdom?

What does it tell us about his power?

What gives us confidence that this will be the future of the church of Jesus Christ (v 7)?

What does it mean for you personally to look forward to being part of this kingdom for ever?

➔ apply

4. The glorious, eternal kingdom seen by John in Revelation 5 is the church. What practical difference should that make in our attitude towards our local church?

⊡ getting personal

Reflect on these implications of belonging to God's kingdom of priests from every nation:

- *When your church seems disappointing, difficult or dull, how will you remember that they are part of the cosmically and eternally significant kingdom of God?*

- *Since God's kingdom is from all nations, what work will you support to bring the gospel to a group of unreached people, whether local or far away?*

- *How can you contribute to making the message of Jesus known so that people can join his kingdom?*

- *As someone in God's kingdom of priests, how are you serving him in your church right now?*

⊕ investigate

▶ Read Matthew 28:16-20

These last-recorded words of Jesus in Matthew's Gospel before his ascension are known as the Great Commission.

5. Jesus is the King of God's kingdom. What is king-like about the way he speaks here?

DICTIONARY

Disciple (v 16): someone who learns from a master.

Baptising (v 19): symbolic washing of someone who has come to trust in Jesus for salvation and a sign of joining the church.

6. How does he command his disciples to build the kingdom?

• How do we know that these commands are for disciples today too?

7. What feature of God's kingdom which we have already seen in Revelation 5 is mentioned here as well?

8. How is Jesus' strategy different from the normal ways in which kings build a kingdom? (Compare Luke 22:47-51; Romans 16:17-18; 1 Thessalonians 2:3-5.)

• In what way would this have seemed like a crazy ambition and a hopeless mission?

9. What does Jesus say to give his disciples confidence as they face this enormous task?

⊖ **apply**

10. In what ways does Jesus' Great Commission still seem like a crazy ambition and a hopeless mission today?

11. "My kingdom is not of this world," Jesus says to Pilate in John 18:36. In what ways today can churches forget these words?

⊕ **pray**

"Our Father in heaven, hallowed be your name, *your kingdom come,* your will be done, on earth as it is in heaven." (Matthew 6:9-10)

Make this the centre of your prayers together, informed by what you have learned about God's kingdom and how he is building it.

3 Mark 3:20-35; Matthew 10:32-42
GOD'S FAMILY

⊕ talkabout

1. Mention two people who are important to you and briefly explain their importance:

   • A family member—whether a biological, adoptive, foster or honorary relative, and whether or not they are still living.

   • A fellow Christian—perhaps someone who led you to Christ or has been significant in discipling you.

⊕ investigate

❯ Read Mark 3:20-35

2. In verse 21, why do you think Jesus' family had decided that he was out of his mind?

   • What did they want to do, and what was their motivation, do you think?

DICTIONARY

Beelzebul (v 22): another name for Satan. **Blaspheme against the Holy Spirit (v 29):** when someone so stubbornly resists the Spirit convicting them of the truth and their need of the gospel that he withdraws for ever, and so they are never able to repent and be forgiven.

3. What evidence in verses 22-27 shows that the family's view of Jesus was totally inappropriate? (Think about what Jesus has been doing and with what power he's been doing it.)

4. How does Jesus then redefine his family, and what is his purpose in doing that, do you think?

- **Read Luke 8:19-21.** How do Jesus' words here explain what he means by "whoever does God's will"?

5. In Mark 3, compare where Jesus' true family are (v 34) with where his biological family are (v 31-32); then compare what both groups are doing.

- Why does Jesus prioritise the former?

6. **Read 1 Thessalonians 2:6-12.** In what ways does Paul view and treat fellow Christians as his family, just as Jesus did?

optional

⊡ explore more

The theme of God's family can be traced from the Old Testament through the whole Bible.

> **Read Exodus 4:19-23 and Galatians 6:14-16**

In Exodus 4, whom does God call "my son"? And how is this developed in Galatians 6?

> **Read God's promise to King David in 2 Samuel 7:11b-14a, and Hebrews 1:1-5**

In 2 Samuel 7, whom does God call "my son"? And how is this developed in Hebrews 1?

> **Read 1 John 3:7-10**

What is the link between the children of God and the Son of God?

Is everyone a child of God? If not, who is and who isn't?

⊡ apply

7. If the church is our family, what privileges and responsibilities does that bring? How should this shape our attitudes and actions?

• How could you help your church feel more like a family?

"As we have opportunity, let us do good to all people, especially to those who belong to the family of believers." (Galatians 6:10)

In what ways are you doing good especially to the family of believers? What good could you do *this week*?

If you are stuck for ideas about how to follow this command, who could you talk to about it?

⊥ investigate

> ❯ **Read Matthew 10:32-42**

8. If we would follow Jesus, what is to be our priority throughout life (v 32-33)?

DICTIONARY

Take up their cross (v 38): Jesus calls his followers to be ready to die, even shamefully, for him.

9. What will often prevent people from acknowledging Jesus as Lord and Saviour (v 34-36)?

• To overcome this, what attitude do we Christians need (v 37-38)?

• What does Jesus promise for those who persevere (v 39)?

10. How important to Jesus are his family of followers, and how does he show his closeness to us (v 40-42)?

⤷ apply

11. In what ways have you seen allegiance to family put above allegiance to Jesus? (Perhaps you yourself have done this.)

• What are the consequences for the gospel and our church?

12. How can this study encourage followers of Jesus who have an unbelieving family?

⊡ getting personal

"No one who has left home or brothers or sisters or mother or father or children or fields for me and the gospel will fail to receive a hundred times as much in this present age: homes, brothers, sisters, mothers, children and fields—along with persecutions—and in the age to come eternal life." (Mark 10:29-30)

Do you trust Jesus enough to seek his kingdom first, and put your family second to Jesus? Do you trust that this will be best for both your family and yourself?

What changes do you need to make right now to ensure that Jesus has first place in your heart and life?

⬆ pray

"See what great love the Father has lavished on us, that we should be called children of God!" (1 John 3:1)

Let this truth shape your prayers of thanks and your requests to our heavenly Father.

4 GOD'S TEMPLE

Ephesians 2:11-22; 2 Corinthians 6:14 – 7:1

⊕ talkabout

1. Where do people today expect to find God? How near to or far from the truth would you say these ideas were?

• What do you know about the Jerusalem Temple?

optional

⋮ explore more

❯ **Read Psalm 27:1-6**

Find three ways in which the temple/house/tent of the Lord was significant for David. (Note: The permanent temple in Jerusalem was not built until the reign of David's son Solomon. At this time a tent or tabernacle was used.)
• *v 4*
• *v 5*
• *v 6*

In the New Testament the church is described as the temple of God. In what ways does church enable people to find God and enjoy being with him, be kept safe from our enemies, and offer sacrifices to him?

⊡ investigate

❯ Read Ephesians 2:11-22

Here Paul addresses Gentile (non-Jewish) Christians. Gentiles were despised by Jewish people for being "uncircumcised" (v 11). Though previously Gentile Christians had not enjoyed the privileges that God granted to Israel (v 12), Paul shows that Christ has done for Gentiles exactly what he has done for Jews. In Christ Gentiles have the same status and blessings as ethnically Jewish Christians (v 13-18). Paul pictures both Jewish and Gentile Christians together being built into God's temple (v 19-22).

2. What do you think is meant by "the foundation of the apostles and prophets" (v 20)?

3. Reread verses 14-18. How has Jesus fulfilled the function of the chief cornerstone in his church?

4. Find three things that verse 21 tells us about all Christian believers.

5. What are the implications of verse 22? Think about...
  • our privilege (see 1 Kings 8:27-29 and 9:3)

  • our mission (see 1 Kings 8:41-43)

☐→ apply

6. What part can we play in ensuring that our church...
  • is "built on the foundation of the apostles and prophets"?

  • is "joined together" in Jesus our cornerstone?

☺ getting personal

"In [Christ] you too are being built together to become a dwelling in which God lives by his Spirit." (Ephesians 2:22)

Think of one or two ways in which this truth will affect how you go to church, how you treat Christians there and how you get involved in church activities.

⊕ investigate

> **❯ Read 2 Corinthians 6:14 – 7:1**

7. How does Paul contrast believers and unbelievers? Complete the table.

VERSE	BELIEVERS	UNBELIEVERS
14		
14		
15		
16		

8. "Do not be yoked together with unbelievers." Does Paul's instruction here mean believers should have no contact whatever with unbelievers? (See 1 Corinthians 5:9-10.)

• What kind of partnerships does Paul have in mind, do you think?

9. Since we are "the temple of the living God", what four things must we do (6:17 x 3 and 7:1)? And what will each look like?

- What promises are we given that spur us to do these things (v 16, 18)?

10. In practice, what does it look like for a church to purify themselves?

- Matthew 18:15-17

- Galatians 6:1

- 2 Thessalonians 3:6, 14-15

- 1 Corinthians 5:12-13

→ apply

11. Discuss a lifelike situation in which a believer is yoked together with an unbeliever. How might you and your church need to respond?

12. Why is it so difficult for us to keep the church of Christ pure?

- What are some of the potential consequences if we fail to purify ourselves as a church?

⊡ getting personal

"Let us purify ourselves from everything that contaminates body and spirit, perfecting holiness out of reverence for God." (2 Corinthians 7:1)

How much is "perfecting holiness" part of your life, both personally and in your church? Is this something you really need to get started on? How can you tell if you're doing this with wrong motives—to justify yourself or look good in the eyes of others rather than "out of reverence for God"? How will knowing that you are part of the temple of the living God help you to live for purity?

⊙ pray

Confess to God ways in which you have allowed yourself to be contaminated by sinful influences, people, desires, reactions and motives, and ask God's forgiveness for each one.

Ask God to help you and your church be joined together and built up on the foundation of his word; and pray especially for the leaders among you who are responsible for teaching and applying God's word.

5 CHRIST'S BODY

1 Corinthians 12; Ephesians 4:1-7, 11-16

⊕ talkabout

1. In what ways is your church a diverse group of people?

   • In what ways is your church a united group of people?

⊕ investigate

> **▶ Read 1 Corinthians 12:1-31**

2. Look at verses 4-14. What type of differences within a church does Paul highlight in verses 4-6? What (or rather, who) is the reason behind this diversity?

   • What reason does Paul give for the unity of God's people?

> **DICTIONARY**
>
> **Pagans (v 2):** those who worship false gods.
> **Manifestation (v 7):** a gift or work of the Spirit in someone that others can see.
> **Tongues (v 10):** languages. Christians differ on whether these are human or angelic.
> **Apostles (v 28):** those sent out with the good news of Jesus Christ.
> **Prophets (v 28):** those who communicate God's word (e.g. 1 Corinthians 14:3); probably includes preaching, exhorting and sharing from Scripture.

3. What is the purpose for which the Spirit gives God's people various gifts (v 7)? What can go wrong if we forget this purpose?

4. What are the implications of the fact that Christ's church is like a body for when...
   • you feel different to everyone else (v 15-20)?

   • someone else is different to you (v 21-26)?

5. What kind of people might Paul have in mind when he mentions those who "seem to be weaker" (v 22), or that "we think are less honourable", or are "unpresentable" (v 23)?

   • How does Paul view such people in the body of Christ (v 22-23)?

   • What clues does the passage give about how we should treat such people?

6. Look at verses 27-31. What are "the greater gifts"? Why are they called that, do you think?

How is it that Paul tells us to "eagerly desire the greater gifts", yet also that we are not all given the same gifts (v 29)? We'll struggle to square this circle if we think individualistically, forgetting that the church is one body. We are not all to eagerly desire the greater gifts for ourselves; instead we eagerly desire them for the body, because we know it's absolutely essential that our church has these gifts.

⊕ **apply**

7. From this passage, how would you try to help...
  • someone who is convinced that God has called them to be a Bible teacher?
  • someone who is upset that that they haven't been chosen for the "worship-leader" rota, insisting that this is their special gift?
  • someone who believes they have nothing to contribute in church?
  • someone who is embarrassed to be paired with an elderly woman on the church welcome team?

8. What kind of people might be viewed as weak, less honourable or unpresentable in your church?

  • What would it look like to treat people from these categories with special honour?

"There are different kinds of working, but in all of them and in everyone it is the same God at work." (1 Corinthians 12:6)

How do you think God might currently be working through you? And how much do you expect and trust God to be at work through your brothers and sisters in Christ? What things can you thank him for that he has been doing through them and you?

⊌ **investigate**

▶ **Read Ephesians 4:1-7, 11-16**

DICTIONARY

Evangelists (v 11): those gifted in sharing the good news of Jesus with unbelievers.
Pastors (v 11): literally, "shepherds"; those gifted in leading and giving spiritual care to believers in a church.

9. *Unity* (verses 1-6): How has God produced unity in the body of Christ?

• What responsibility regarding our unity is given to believers in the body of Christ?

10. *Diversity* (verses 11-12): Two tasks are mentioned for which Christ apportions grace (v 7) to all believers.
    • What is the task of those given the gifts described in verse 11?

    • What is the task of all the other believers (v 12)?

- What is the one purpose that all work towards (end of v 12)?

11. *Maturity* (verses 13-16). Maturity among God's people means becoming increasingly like Jesus Christ—"attaining to the whole measure of the fullness of Christ" (v 13) and becoming "in every respect the mature body of him who is the head, that is, Christ" (v 15). What does it look like when we are mature...

- in our faith (v 13-14)?

- in our relationships with fellow believers (v 15)?

- in our commitment to our church (v 16)?

□□ **explore more**

❯ **Read Psalm 133**

In this psalm, oil and dew are associated with unity.

Oil (v 2): This was used in the Old Testament to consecrate priests for their work of serving God in the temple.

Where does the oil flow from and to? How does this relate to what we've seen in Ephesians 4:15?

Why is oil such a good picture of unity? (see Psalm 23:5; 45:7; 104:15)?

Dew (v 3): The high peak of Mount Hermon was in the far north of Israel, about 250 miles from Mount Zion in Jerusalem, the place signifying God's people in the Old Testament. Hermon receives plentiful dew all year due to its coastal climate. Zion, however, is part of a limestone plateau so surface water is scarce, and the rains there are less frequent. For the dew of Mount Hermon to fall on Mount Zion would require a miracle!

What does this tell us about unity?

Think about your experiences of the unity of God's people. How do they match the truths expressed in this psalm?

⮕ apply

12. How do "those parts of the body that seem to be weaker" (1 Corinthians 12:22) help the whole body to increasingly mature in Christ-likeness?

• What could this look like in practice in your church?

☺ getting personal

"Speaking the truth in love, we will grow to become in every respect the mature body of ... Christ." (Ephesians 4:15)

In what parts of your life together in your church do you think you might lack maturity (i.e. Christ-likeness)? Is there some way in which you can help your church to mature by speaking the truth in love?

⬆ pray

Review what you have learned in this study; find one thing to thank God for and one thing which you need to ask for his help with.

6 Ephesians 5:25-33; 2 Corinthians 11:1-15
CHRIST'S BRIDE

⊕ talkabout

1. Think of some films, books, TV dramas or stage shows which end with a marriage. How do those kind of endings make you feel—jubilant or cynical? Why, do you think?

⊙ investigate

> **Read Ephesians 5:25-32**

2. What or who is the original model in this passage, and what or who is the copy?

DICTIONARY

Mystery (v 32): something that was not understood in the past but has now been revealed.

3. List the things that Christ has done (past) for his bride, the church (v 25-26).

• For what purpose (v 27)?

4. List the things that Christ is doing now (present) for his bride, the church (v 26-27, 29).

- What words here describe the kind of church that Christ will produce?

optional

🙂 explore more

Ephesians 5 isn't the first time in the Bible that marriage is used as a picture of the relationship between God's people and God.

❯ Read Isaiah 54:1-8

God describes himself as a husband (v 5), and his "wife" is the people of God: Israel.

What has this "wife" suffered in her previous experience of "marriage" with another "husband"?
- *v 1*
- *v 4 (see also v 6)*
- *v 4 again*

The woman representing Israel is no longer in a marriage where she is sinned against; she is now the wife of her Maker. But how do we know that in this utterly different and incomparably better marriage, she herself has sinned (v 7-8)? What could she have been guilty of?

In the Bible a husband's jealousy at a wife's adultery frequently pictures God's response to the idolatry of his people—when they turn elsewhere than to God for protection, provision and fulfilment (for example, Jeremiah 3:6, 12-13). But these "gods" are powerless to provide what we need. The inevitable consequences of idolatry are seen in the wife's suffering both before and during her marriage with her Maker in Isaiah 54: fruitlessness like infertility, grief and despair like widowhood, pain like rejection, and aloneness like desertion.

How is God's graciousness seen in Isaiah 54, in the face of this adultery/idolatry?

"If you belong to Christ, then you are Abraham's seed, and heirs according to the promise" (Galatians 3:29). God's New Testament people, the church, share in God's promises to Israel. So Isaiah 54 is a picture of the future for all God's people in marriage to their Maker.

Looking again at those verses, what will our future be like?

⊡ apply

5. God's people collectively are the bride of Christ. How will this change the way you view church?

• How will it better motivate you to live for Jesus Christ?

⊡ getting personal

"Then I heard ... 'Hallelujah! ... For the wedding of the Lamb has come, and his bride has made herself ready. Fine linen, bright and clean, was given her to wear.' (Fine linen stands for the righteous acts of God's holy people.)" (Revelation 19:6-8)

We all have a part to play in making the bride ready for the wedding of the Lamb. What could you do this week to encourage others to dress in the clothing that we have been "given ... to wear"? And what righteous acts do you think God has given you to do?

⊕ investigate

❯ Read 2 Corinthians 11:1-15

6. What is Paul's goal for the Corinthian Christians (v 2)?

• What does it mean in practice to be a "pure virgin" here (v 3)?

7. Who could derail Paul's objective, and how could they do that (v 3, v 4, v 5)?

8. How precisely can false teachers deceive us (v 13-15)?

• What are the implications of this?

9. How can we spot false teachers (v 5-11)?

• How can we avoid being taken in?

→ **apply**

10. What might it look like to support the ongoing work in your church of presenting Christ's people as a pure virgin to their husband?

⊡ **getting personal**

Use these questions to review your vulnerability to deception.

• What impressive appearances might deceive you?

• How carefully do you listen and hold to the apostolic message?

• What could be causing you to be insincere or impure in your devotion to Christ?

↑ **pray**

"The Spirit and the bride say, 'Come!' ... He who testifies to these things says, 'Yes, I am coming soon.' Amen. Come, Lord Jesus."

(Revelation 22:17, 20)

As you pray for Jesus' return, thank God that the ultimate wedding day is coming soon. Ask him to help you...

• grow in sincere and pure devotion to Jesus the Bridegroom.

• clothe yourself with the righteousness of Christ, in faith and in deeds, as you make yourself ready for him on that day.

• stay faithful to Jesus through difficult times now in certain hope of the approaching "happily-ever-after" ending for all his people .

7 Ephesians 2:1-10; 3:2-11
GOD'S MASTERPIECE

⊕ talkabout

1. What are the big "stories" or causes, if any, that people seek to live for—things that are bigger and will last longer than themselves?

- What kinds of things limit the grandeur of these "bigger stories"?

⊕ investigate

❯ Read Ephesians 2:1-10

Paul is describing the journey of all true followers of Jesus: the past that we all share, the process we have all been through and the position we now enjoy.

2. List all the things in verses 1-3 that Christians ("you") did or were.

DICTIONARY

Transgressions (v 1): a false step; wrongdoing that can be relatively non-deliberate.
Ruler of the kingdom of the air (v 2): Satan.
Flesh (v 3): the sinful nature that we are all born with.
Wrath (v 3): God's response of righteous anger to sin.
Works (v 9, 10): in v 9, things we do by which we hope to earn God's favour; in v 10, things we do that reflect God's character.

- "You were *dead* in your transgressions and sins, in which you used to *live*" (v 1-2). What does Paul mean by "dead", and what are the implications of this?

3. List all the things in verses 4-10 that God did and has done for his people.

- What is the connection between Jesus Christ and the people that God saves through him?

4. What do these two lists together (questions 2 and 3) reveal about God's character?

- Looking at these verses, what characteristics will mark God's people in Christ?

5. What will be the effect of Christ's church in this world (v 7)?

• What part do his people play to bring this about (v 10)?

optional

⊡ explore more

❯ **Read Isaiah 11:1-10**

How does this Old Testament prophecy reflect some of the things that we have learned about the church of Christ so far (in this session or previous ones)?

⊖ apply

6. "We are God's handiwork, created in Christ Jesus to do good works, which God prepared in advance for us to do" (Ephesians 2:10). What does this look like in your church, and in your life?

• How do we make sure that it's God's incomparable grace that is displayed through our good deeds?

⊡ getting personal

"Jesus Christ ... gave himself for us to redeem us from all wickedness and to purify for himself a people that are his very own, eager to do what is good" (Titus 2:13-14).

The way to be eager to do good begins with understanding and marvelling at what Jesus Christ has done for us. Perhaps you feel that you need to grow in your eagerness to do good. Take time to reflect on how Jesus has redeemed you from wickedness and purified you to belong to him and do the good works that God has prepared for you.

⊕ investigate

❯ Read Ephesians 3:2-11

7. Paul talks in these verses about a "mystery"—a big truth that God did not reveal to his people before the age of the apostles, but which Paul is now proclaiming to the church at Ephesus. What is it (v 6)?

8. What, then, is unique about the message of the gospel and the church that it produces?

9. What will be the effect of Christ's church on the entire cosmos (v 10-11)?

⤷ apply

The church is what reveals God's multi-coloured wisdom to the entire cosmos—not only to humans but to spiritual rulers and authorities in the heavenly realms—and will do so eternally. This is the bigger story that we have the privilege of being part of!

10. When is it hard to remember that the church is God's masterpiece to display his glory to the cosmos?

- At those times, how can we help one another to lift our eyes to what God is doing through his church?

11. What excites you most about this idea of the church as God's masterpiece? In what ways is it better than the other "bigger stories" you talked about in question 1?

⬚ getting personal

> "Most of us go through day after day and seldom feel the impact
> of the magnitude of what we are caught up in by belonging to
> Jesus Christ, the God-Man, the ruler of the universe. And we don't
> take enough time to meditate on how our jobs, our home life, our
> leisure, our church involvement—how each of these fits into the
> cosmic significance of the church. And consequently our lives often
> lack the flavour of eternity and the aroma of something ultimate."
> (John Piper, www.desiringgod.org/messages/the-cosmic-church)

In what ways might you personally need to elevate your commitment
to and love for your church to better reflect God's cosmic purposes
for his gathered people in Christ? What might that look like this
week?

⬆ pray

> *"Now to him who is able to do immeasurably more than all we ask or
> imagine, according to his power that is at work within us, to him be
> glory in the church and in Christ Jesus throughout all generations, for
> ever and ever! Amen." (Ephesians 3:20-21)*

Praise God for the privilege of being part of this "big story". Pray
specifically for things that will enable your church to bring God glory on
earth and in heaven throughout all generations, thanking him for his
immeasurable and unimaginable power at work within you and your
fellow believers.

8 Acts 6:1-7; Acts 8 and 11
CHURCH IN THIS WORLD

⊕ talkabout

1. What kinds of things sometimes make our experience of church disappointing or difficult?

In the previous seven sessions we have seen God's intimate love and cosmic purposes for the church of Christ. Nevertheless, the day-to-day experience of life in a local church can often be difficult and disappointing. This was even true of the first church in Jerusalem.

⊕ investigate

> **▶ Read Acts 6:1-7**

2. What problem emerged in the first church in Jerusalem?

DICTIONARY

Hellenistic (v 1): Jewish people whose culture and first language was Greek. **Hebraic (v 1):** Jewish people whose first language was Aramaic; not culturally Greek.

• What caused this problem, do you think?

3.   What dilemma did this problem present to the apostles?

• How would ignoring the problem have affected the church's gospel ministry?

4.   What was so good about the solution the apostles came up with?

• How does it illustrate the importance of the church acting as a body (see Session 5)?

5.   What snippets of godly wisdom for church life can we learn from this story?

6.   What was the effect of sorting out the church's problem, according to Luke (v 7)?

⊡ apply

7. What divisions could occur in your church family?

• How could you help the leaders in your church to overcome these sorts of problems?

⊡ investigate

The rest of Acts 6 and 7 describe how Stephen, one of the seven chosen in 6:5, was arrested and stoned to death by the Jewish leaders for preaching about Jesus.

❯ Read Acts 8:1-4 and 11:19-21

In these two passages we see the first single church of Jewish believers in Jerusalem grow into a church of multiple groups of believers located in many different places.

8. What were the means by which the church grew?

DICTIONARY

Judea and Samaria (8:1): regions of Israel; the Jewish heartland and the more pagan area to the north.
Saul (v 3): a highly educated religious Jew whose mission was to destroy Christianity; later converted and became Paul (Acts 9).
Phoenicia, Cyprus and Antioch (11:19): places in the eastern Mediterranean area.
Greeks (v 20): Greek-speaking (Hellenistic) Jewish people.

▸ Read Acts 11:22-26

DICTIONARY

Barnabas (v 22): a leading believer first mentioned in Acts 4:36-37. **Tarsus (v 25):** Saul's home city in modern-day south-central Turkey.

9. What were the means by which the new church at Antioch was established?

10. After these events, how might faithful believers have viewed persecution, do you think?

⊖ apply

11. What persecution could your church face? How might God use that, do you think?

   • How can you help fellow believers to remain true to the Lord when your church faces hostility and opposition?

12. What have you learned, in this session and all of these studies, that will help you to stick with your brothers and sisters in Christ and remain true to the Lord with all your heart?

⊕ pray

Jesus promised, "I will build my church, and the gates of Hades [the power of death] will not overcome it" (Matthew 16:18).

- Thank God that because Christ has promised this, it will take place.

- Thank God specifically for what that means for you and your particular church, in light of all that we have learned about the church from God's word.

- Ask God to help you, when your church is difficult or disappointing, to not give up meeting with your brothers and sisters in Christ and to remain true to the Lord as you keep serving him among his people.

Leader's Guide

INTRODUCTION

Leading a Bible study can be a bit like herding cats—everyone has a different idea of what the passage could be about, and a different line of enquiry that they want to pursue. But a good group leader is more than someone who just referees this kind of discussion. You will want to:

- correctly understand and handle the Bible passage. But also...

- encourage and train the people in your group to do this for themselves. Don't fall into the trap of spoon-feeding people by simply passing on the information in the Leader's Guide. Then...

- make sure that no Bible study is finished without everyone knowing how the passage is relevant for them. What changes do you all need to make in the light of the things you have been learning? And finally...

- encourage the group to turn all that has been learned and discussed into prayer.

Your Bible-study group is unique, and you are likely to know better than anyone the capabilities, backgrounds and circumstances of the people you are leading. That's why we've designed these guides with a number of optional features. If they're a quiet bunch, you might want to spend longer on *talkabout*. If your time is limited, you can choose to skip *explore more*, or get people to look at these questions at home. Can't get enough of Bible study? Well, some studies have optional extra homework projects. As leader, you can adapt and select the material to the needs of your particular group.

So what's in the Leader's Guide? The main thing that this Leader's Guide will help you to do is to understand the major teaching points in the passage you are studying, and how to apply them. As well as guidance for the questions, the Leader's Guide for each session contains the following important sections:

THE BIG IDEA

One or two key sentences will give you the main point of the session. This is what you should be aiming to have fixed in people's minds as they leave the Bible study. And it's the point you need to head back toward when the discussion goes off at a tangent.

SUMMARY

An overview of the passage, including plenty of useful historical background information.

OPTIONAL EXTRA

Usually this is an introductory activity that ties in with the main theme of the Bible study, and is designed to "break the ice" at the beginning of a session. Or it may be a "homework project" that people can tackle during the week.

So let's take a look at the various different features of a Good Book Guide:

⊕ talkabout

Each session kicks off with a discussion question, based on the group's opinions or experiences. It's designed to get people talking and thinking in a general way about the main subject of the Bible study.

⬇ investigate

The first thing you and your group need to know is what the Bible passage is about, which is the purpose of these questions. But watch out—people may come up with answers based on their experiences or teaching they have heard in the past, without referring to the passage at all. It's amazing how often we can get through a Bible study without actually looking at the Bible! If you're stuck for an answer, the Leader's Guide contains guidance for questions. These are the answers to direct your group to. This information isn't meant to be read out to people—ideally, you want them to discover these answers from the Bible for themselves. Sometimes there are optional follow-up questions (see ☑ in guidance for questions) to help you help your group get to the answer.

⊡ explore more

These questions generally point people to other relevant parts of the Bible. They are useful for helping your group to see how the passage fits into the "big picture" of the whole Bible. These sections are OPTIONAL—only use them if you have time. Remember that it's better to finish in good time having really grasped one big thing from the passage, than to try and cram everything in.

⤳ apply

We want to encourage you to spend more time working at application—too often, it is simply tacked on at the end. In the Good Book Guides, apply sections are mixed in with the investigate sections of the study. We hope that people will realize that application is not just an optional extra, but rather, the whole purpose of studying the

Bible. We do Bible study so that our lives can be changed by what we hear from God's word. If you skip the application, the Bible study hasn't achieved its purpose.

These questions draw out practical lessons that we can all learn from the Bible passage. You can review what has been learned so far, and think about practical differences that this should make in our churches and our lives. The group gets the opportunity to talk about what they personally have learned.

⊡ getting personal

These can be done at home, but it is well worth allowing a few moments of quiet reflection during the study for each person to think and pray about specific changes they need to make in their own lives. Why not have a time for reporting back at the beginning of the following session, so that everyone can be encouraged and challenged by one another to make application a priority?

⬆ pray

In Acts 4:25-30 the first Christians quoted Psalm 2 as they prayed in response to the persecution of the apostles by the Jewish religious leaders. Today however, it's not as common for Christians to base prayers on the truths of God's word as it once was. As a result, our prayers tend to be weak, superficial and self-centred rather than bold, visionary and God-centred.

The prayer section is based on what has been learned from the Bible passage. How different our prayer times would be if we were genuinely responding to what God has said to us through his word.

1

1 Peter 1 and 2; Acts 2:42-47
GOD'S PEOPLE

THE BIG IDEA

A church isn't a building, denomination or Sunday services. It's people—chosen, saved and sanctified by the triune God, to be both scattered exiles in this world and the royalty of the universe, and seen in local gatherings.

SUMMARY

In the Bible, the word "church" has two meanings: (1) all believers everywhere throughout history, and (2) a local group of believers. While most people today think of "church" very differently—usually as a building—it is always a gathering of people in the New Testament.

This study explores the New Testament sense of "church"—first, by examining two parts of Peter's first letter to churches in what is now Turkey; and second, by reading about the first church, in Jerusalem.

In his letters, Peter never uses the word "church", but the greeting in 1 Peter makes clear that he was writing to multiple churches throughout Asia Minor (what is Turkey today). Other New Testament letter greetings are similar (1 Corinthians 1:2; 2 Corinthians 1:1, James 1:1), so it's reasonable to think that Peter's descriptions of his Christian readers aren't specific to the churches he addresses, and can be applied to us today.

He shows a sharp contrast between how the world views these Christians and their status in God's eyes. Unbelievers think Christians are scattered exiles—weak, insignificant outsiders—but in fact they're God's elect: chosen by him, sanctified by the Spirit,

and sprinkled (made holy) with the blood of Jesus. In 1 Peter 2, Peter goes further: these churches are "a chosen people, a royal priesthood, a holy nation" and "God's special possession".

In Acts 2 we see the very first Jerusalem church: 3,000+ people who gathered daily, despite having no public premises of their own, and who were devoted to the apostles' teaching, fellowship, the breaking of bread (meals together and the Lord's Supper) and prayer; and were marked by giving, sharing and pastoral care which ensured that no one among them was left in need. How closely do our churches, and our views of church, reflect Peter's teaching and that first church in Jerusalem?

OPTIONAL EXTRA

(Goes with question 1) Start with a drawing competition, for individuals or teams. Provide paper and pens, set a time limit and tell your group to draw a church. This will reveal how people think of a church. How many will draw a building and not people? Give prizes for any picture of people.

GUIDANCE FOR QUESTIONS

1. What comes to mind when you hear the word "church"? (If you've done the Optional Extra activity, ask about the views of non-churchgoers.) Most people think of a religious building. Some think of a denomination, or a Sunday service ("I'll see you at church tomorrow"). However, our word "church" translates the Greek word ekklesia: a gathering of people. (You'll return to this discussion in question 9.)

2. How does Peter describe the people he is writing to?

- Verse 1: "God's elect"—chosen by him to be saved from sin (also v 2).
- "Exiles"—in this case scattered across modern-day Turkey. Where they currently live is not their true home; their roots aren't there. Peter probably wrote to ethnically Jewish Christians exiled from Judea, but all followers of Jesus share the experience of "exile". Our citizenship is in heaven (Philippians 3:20); that is our true home. (To unpack "exile", ask people to share "exile" experiences or stories they know of migrants or refugees.)
- Verse 2: They are being sanctified (made holy) by the work of the Spirit.
- God's purpose is for them to be "obedient to Jesus Christ"; he is their Lord.
- They have been "sprinkled with [Jesus'] blood"—cleansed and made acceptable for God's presence by the death of Jesus.

- **What's comforting and what's challenging about his description?**
  Comforting: The work of the triune God for us, in us and on our behalf. The Father has chosen us; Jesus has sprinkled us with his blood; and the Spirit sanctifies us. Things that we could never do ourselves— being cleansed from sin, becoming acceptable to God, becoming holy— have been done for us by God himself. *Challenging:* In this world we are exiles— we mustn't make a home for ourselves here; we will always feel somewhat out of place. And we are scattered—Jesus' true church will never be seen by unbelievers as powerfully united and numerically strong because our connectedness is invisible. It is as weak outsiders that we're called to be obedient to Jesus.

3. How does Peter's description contrast with commonly-held views in our culture today of what a church is?

Work through each description highlighted in the first part of question 2 and think about how people see the church differently.

- *"God's elect" (v 1)* and *"chosen [by] God the Father (v 2):* People think church is a club for self-selecting religious people. Some Christians, too, see church as something they choose to join rather than the people that God has chosen and qualified them to be.
- *"Exiles" and "scattered" (v 1):* Some (e.g. traditionalists or non-Westerners) see church as part of a so-called "Christian society", and not as exiles in that society. Others view church as part of the machinery of power that suppresses liberalism, and not as scattered people lacking power and influence. Many think the church is only Western (and dying); they're unaware that Christians are scattered everywhere and are mostly in the majority (developing) world.
- *Those who experience "the sanctifying work of the Spirit":* People think churchgoers claim to live good lives, believing they are better than others, and so, at worst, they're self-righteous, judgmental and hypocritical. True Christianity teaches that believers are as sinful as anyone, and only the work of the Spirit in our lives can make us in any way good.
- *"To be obedient to Jesus Christ" (v 2):* Views on why people belong to church include: to express national or cultural identity, keep traditions alive, make friends in a local community, because of upbringing, to connect with the transcendent, as an insurance for the afterlife, to give children morality guidance, etc. All these ideas miss the reason for the church that Peter highlights here.

- *"Sprinkled with [Jesus'] blood" (v 2):*
  Clearly from Peter's description, joining the church is not the result of our choice and actions. None of us have any right to be part of God's elect people. Inclusion comes only through the cleansing of our sins, which comes only through faith in what Jesus achieved by his death on the cross.

4. Peter previously described the followers of Jesus as "scattered". Here, how are we united? (Think about our identity and our role.)

- A "people" and a "nation" (v 9, 10)—we're united by sharing an identity, a history and a culture. As God made Abraham's descendants into a people and nation when he rescued them from Egypt (Exodus 6:2-8, especially v 7), he has given followers of Jesus a common identity and history by rescuing us from sin and judgment.
- A "royal priesthood" (1 Peter 2 v 9)—we're united by our role and purpose. As Old Testament priests taught people about God and helped them come to God in the required way (through offering sacrifices), followers of Jesus declare God's praises and his salvation to others, so that they too can come to him in the required way—through faith in Jesus.

5. Peter previously described the followers of Jesus as "exiles" ... Here, what shows our privileged status? Far

from appearances in this world, followers of Jesus have the highest status possible: we've been "chosen" by God himself; we are described as "royal" and "holy" (set apart for God); God considers us as his "special possession" (v 9). None of this is achieved by our goodness or efforts. It's all the result of God's mercy (v 10).

6. What do we learn here about...
- **our relationship with God?** We've been chosen by God himself; we're "royal" because we're now in the family of the King of the universe; we're God's "special possession"—like his Old Testament people, Israel (Exodus 19:5)—so more than simply part of his creation; God called us out of darkness *to himself*; scattered sinful individuals have become "the people of God"; we have now received his mercy. (Perhaps pause to offer God some thanks and praise.)

- **our mission in this world?** To declare God's praises, now that we've experienced his mercy and grace.

- **the contrast between our past and our present?** Followers of Jesus are not born that way but all come from a dark past (v 9). All true Christians have a story of "Once... but now..." (v 10).

EXPLORE MORE [Psalm 68:1-10, 32-35]
Verses 1-3 ... How are God's enemies described? As those who are "wicked" (v 2)—or "rebellious" (v 6)—who will flee from God and perish. (*Note:* Here (v 1) to be "scattered" is part of God's judgment. However, for a limited time and because of the Great Commission (see Session 2), God has allowed his people today to be scattered.)

What marks out his people here? They are righteous; and their response to God is joy, not terror. (*Note:* Here, inclusion among God's people is not based on Israelite nationality but on righteousness. Although in Old Testament history, Israel enjoyed the special status of God's treasured possession (Exodus 19:5), Paul is clear that not all Israelites were part of God's people (Romans 9:6). God's true people were those who trusted in God and his promises, and were made righteous through their faith (Romans 4:3-5).)

In verses 4-6, what do we learn about God? He is unceasingly active for the good of his people, especially those who are weakest or most wretched. This is the same proactive God as in 1 Peter 1:2.

What do we learn about his people? They are weak and needy but rescued and restored by God, so they praise him with joy—as the church now declares the praises of God (1 Peter 2:9).

From verses 7-10, list the things that God has done in history for his people. Throughout the exodus, God led his people like a general at the head of his army, enduring the same conditions as his men but also enlisting the forces of nature—here, earthquakes and rain; at the exodus, winds and sea (Exodus 14). God was also the provider of abundance and refreshment for his people (Exodus 16:11-35).

What have his people done? God's people simply followed him and enjoyed what he provided. Nothing else was needed because he had done it all.

In verses 32-35 David lists reasons to give God praise and glory. What do God's people contribute? Again, God's people only receive his good gifts and contribute nothing themselves—also a reason for God to be glorified (v 35b).

7. APPLY: What practical difference should both truths [that we are scattered exiles and the astoundingly privileged royalty of the universe] make in our attitude towards Christ's church? Go with the flow of conversation; but here are a few issues you could discuss:

• Is church mainly a building that you visit and look after? Or an organisation that you work for (whether paid or unpaid)? Or just for Sunday?

• Are you dissatisfied with your church because you think it should have a hearing in society, attract influential people, have a better media profile, etc?

• Does increasing hostility towards the Christian faith in Western society make you anxious? Do you fear for the survival of the church in your culture? Is it difficult to trust in God's purposes for his church? Is your confidence to declare God's praises to the world being undermined?

• Is your church central in your life? Is it where you feel most at home, come to be refreshed and find those with whom you have most in common?

8. What essential features of a local church are listed here?

• *People meeting together every day* (v 46a). They did this in the temple courts and in their homes. They already numbered more than 3,000 (2:41), so perhaps they couldn't all meet together at once, but they weren't hindered by the lack of their own building!

• *Devoting themselves to the apostles' teaching.* From the beginning the church had leaders. In this first church, they fulfilled specific criteria (1:21) and were given great power and gifts from God (2:43), to show that they had Jesus' authority (Matthew 28:18-20) and to continue the work he had begun (Acts 1:1). The leaders were responsible for teaching God's people in obedience to Jesus' instructions (Matthew 28:19-20). The apostles' teaching has been preserved for us today in the Bible.

• *Devoting themselves to fellowship.* Believers didn't go to church to meet with God only but with each other as well.

• *Devoting themselves to the breaking of bread*—eating meals together and celebrating the Lord's Supper (v 46b; see

Dictionary, p10).
- *Devoting themselves to prayer.* They met together to do this (Acts 4:23-30; 12:12).
- *Caring for one another* (v 44-45)—not just with nice words but practically and financially, to the extent of sharing property.

9. How would this description of a church surprise people in your culture today, do you think? Compare the previous answer with the views discussed in question 1. This description might surprise even some in your group, as many churches have in some way departed from this description. Indeed, some churches are so far from this description that they are no longer a church in any New Testament sense of that word.

10. APPLY: Read through the features of the first church again. In what ways is your church like this one? Hopefully you will find some similarities. **In what ways is it different? Why, do you think?** Don't let the group simply grumble about your church. The purpose here is to be constructive. No church is perfect and all churches can sometimes be distracted or diverted from the gospel priorities that should shape them.

11. APPLY: How could you help your church to be as much like the first Jerusalem church as possible? There are things that even an ordinary church member can do to teach and model what a New Testament church looks like. Encourage people to think about what they personally can do in your church to encourage devotion to the Bible teaching, to fellowship, to eating together, to prayer and to sharing so that no one among you is in need. How might they change the way they talk to reflect the New

testament meaning of "church"?

- **How would you advise someone whose church does not look in any way like the one described in Acts 2?** As previously mentioned (see note at end of question 9), some churches can no longer really be called a church, especially if there is little or no devotion to the apostles' teaching, since everything in a church flows from the teaching. Sometimes it's time to find a new church.

2 Revelation 5:1-14; Matthew 28:18-20
GOD'S KINGDOM

THE BIG IDEA
The church is God's kingdom, ruled by Christ through his word, and comprising his followers from every nation. It is utterly different from worldly kingdoms, and advanced not by force but by teaching the gospel.

SUMMARY
Jesus began his public ministry by proclaiming, "The kingdom of God has come near. Repent and believe the good news" (Mark 1:15). For centuries the Old Testament had promised a king from David's family whose kingdom would last for ever (2 Samuel 7:11b-13). The New Testament shows that Jesus is the King of God's kingdom—from the records of Jesus' birth (Matthew 2:1-12; Luke 1:26-33), through his teaching about the kingdom, to his trial and crucifixion (John 19:13-22), and here finally in John's vision (Revelation 5). This kingdom is fundamentally different from any in our world; it is, in fact, Christ's church.

This truth should have a transforming effect on the way we view church. God's kingdom is cosmically and eternally significant. There's nothing bigger that we can be part of than Christ's church. Its people come from every tribe, language, people and nation. We are a kingdom of priests who serve God and will reign on the earth, fulfilling God's goal for humanity. Our King is worthy of the adoration not only of his people but of every angel and every creature in creation.

But right now the church neither looks nor feels like that. So we need to trust the final command our King gave while he was on earth: to go and make disciples of people worldwide (Matthew 28:18-20). Knowing how the gospel provokes hostility, ridicule and apathy, we might think this is an ineffective way to advance Christ's kingdom, but this command (not suggestion) is bookended by Christ's assurance of his supreme authority and his promise of his everlasting presence with us as we obey him. Jesus himself said that his kingdom is not of this world (John 18:36). So we need to quash our fears through trusting his promise and the truth about his kingship.

OPTIONAL EXTRA
Organise a fun quiz based on matching kingdoms with their rulers. Ask about fantasy kingdoms from films and books, kingdoms from ancient history or modern "kingdoms" (states and presidents)—or mix it up.

GUIDANCE FOR QUESTIONS
1. What king (or queen) fascinates you and why? (Think past or present, real or fictional!) Get people to share briefly what kingdom (real or fictional) interests them, whether from a museum visit, a holiday, an ancient site, mythology, or a book, film or TV.

- **Would you want to be a citizen of their kingdom? Why or why not?**

2. Who and what is this part of John's vision about? (See especially v 6, 9-10.)
It's about the death of Jesus to save sinners and bring them into the church. The Lamb looks as if he had been slain (v 6) but is now alive again—clearly depicting Jesus,

who died on the cross as a sacrifice for sins (Ephesians 5:2; 2 Corinthians 5:21), and rose from death three days later. With his "blood" he has "purchased" people "for God" (v 9, see 1 Corinthians 6:20; Hebrews 9:12)—meaning that only through Jesus' death on the cross can we live for God and enjoy life now and eternally as one of his children.

3. What do we learn here about God's kingdom?

- **Its people (v 9-10):** (1) They have been purchased by the blood of the Lamb; the way into this kingdom is through the atoning death of Jesus on the cross. (2) They come from every tribe, language, people and nation; the complete range of human cultures is represented in God's kingdom.

- **Its purpose (v 9-10):** This is a kingdom of priests (compare a "royal priesthood", 1 Peter 2:9) with the double role of serving God (under his rule) and reigning on the earth (over the rest of creation). God's original design for humanity (see Genesis 1 and 2; Psalm 8) will be reinstated.

- **Its King (v 11-14):** He is worthy of the adoration not only of his people but of every angel and every creature in creation.

EXPLORE MORE [Isaiah 9 v 2-7]
What does this prophecy tell us about the goodness of the rule of the King of God's kingdom?

- His rule brings people out of deep darkness into great light (v 2). Both Jesus and the apostle John explain that this light is the true, eternal life that only Jesus can give us (John 1:4-9; 8:12).

- His rule brings the defeat of every enemy and everlasting peace (v 3-6). Paul speaks of Jesus' ultimate victory over

the last enemy to be destroyed: death (1 Corinthians 15:20-26).

- Jesus' kingdom will be established and upheld with justice and righteousness (v 7). There will be no more oppressed people or victims of injustice.

What does it tell us about his power? He is named with the titles of God himself (v 6). There can be no more powerful king.

What gives us confidence that this will be the future of the church of Jesus Christ (v 7)? "The zeal of the LORD Almighty will accomplish this." The establishment of this perfectly righteous, supremely victorious, unshakably peaceful, radiantly light-filled, unimaginably endless kingdom is God's passion. It's one thing above everything else that we can be confident about!

What does it mean for you personally to look forward to being part of this kingdom for ever? Hopefully people will have plenty to say here.

4. APPLY: The glorious, eternal kingdom seen by John in Revelation 5 is the church. What practical difference should that make in our attitude towards our local church? Here are some ideas to get the discussion started if needed. (A summary of these is included in the Getting Personal section on p15.)

- God's kingdom is cosmically and eternally significant. There's nothing bigger that we can be part of than Christ's church—something to remember when our own church seems disappointing, difficult or dull.

- God's kingdom is made up of people from every tribe, language, people and nation, so shouldn't we welcome all people in church? Our church should also be involved in reaching unreached groups in some way—whether remote tribes or marginalised people living locally.

- People can only join God's kingdom through the atoning death of Jesus, so making this message known, both inside and outside of church, must be a priority. How can each of us serve this priority?
- Our eternal future in God's kingdom is to serve God, so shouldn't we be doing that now in our church—rather than only doing what we enjoy, or what's good for our children, or what we've always done?

5. Jesus is the King of God's kingdom. What is king-like about the way he speaks here? He has all the authority of heaven and earth (v 18). These words to his disciples are not an option but his command, as is everything that he has told them (v 20). The disciples are to teach throughout the world, with the goal that people who hear will obey Jesus.

6. How does he command his disciples to build the kingdom?

- They have to "go", since Jesus' kingdom comprises people from throughout the world. This won't happen if they just wait for people to come to them.
- They are to make disciples. This isn't a box-ticking exercise, where they simply deliver Jesus' words to every postcode. The disciples need to help people understand the message, its wonder and its urgency, so that they repent and become disciples.
- They are to make disciples by baptising new believers and teaching them to live as followers of Jesus—which means living differently from those around them.

- **How do we know that these commands are for disciples today too?** Jesus' command to make disciples of all nations (v 19) was certainly started by the eleven apostles but continues to this day as an unfinished task. And Jesus' promise

to be with those he has sent to make disciples specifies "to the very end of the age".

7. What feature of God's kingdom which we have already seen in Revelation 5 is mentioned here as well? Again, we see that God's kingdom will comprise people of "all nations" (v 19).

8. How is Jesus' strategy different from the normal ways in which kings build a kingdom? (Compare Luke 22:47-51; Romans 16:17-18; 1 Thessalonians 2:3-5.) Kingdoms in our world are built through force, economic superiority, influence and soft power, or manipulation and deception. Jesus simply gives ordinary people a message to teach to other people. This is done day by day and person by person, as Jesus' followers explain by words and show in their lives who Jesus is and why everyone needs to and can join his kingdom. We can never build his kingdom by using force (Luke 22:47-51) or by deception and manipulation (Romans 16:17-18; 1 Thessalonians 2:3-5).

- **In what way would this have seemed like a crazy ambition and a hopeless mission?** Jesus spoke these words to eleven apostles, and the total number of believers at that time (about 120, Acts 1:15) was fewer than many Sunday congregations today. These were ordinary people with no great education, strength or skills, from a despised ethnic group in an outpost of the Roman Empire. Yet Jesus envisaged such followers making disciples from all nations to the end of history.

9. What does Jesus say to give his disciples confidence as they face this enormous task? All authority in heaven and on earth has been given to Jesus, and he will be with all his disciples in this task

"to the very end of the age". Imagine how confident you would feel carrying a message from the queen marked with her royal crest, written on Buckingham Palace letter paper and signed with her own signature. And if the queen herself accompanied you, surely you would feel completely unassailable.

10. APPLY: In what ways does Jesus' Great Commission still seem like a crazy ambition and a hopeless mission today? Share ways in which you feel the "impossibility" of the Great Commission: you might feel intimidated by hostile Western culture, overwhelmed by the number of unreached people, in despair at people's apathy towards the Christian message, or ill-equipped to tell the gospel. This should be an opportunity to encourage each other with the fortifying promises of Jesus and the comforting truth about his kingship.

11. APPLY: "My kingdom is not of this world," Jesus says to Pilate in John 18:36. In what ways today can churches forget these words? The history of the church has been greatly harmed by attempts to manipulate, cajole or even coerce people into Christ's kingdom, through wars, laws, mobs, taxes, propaganda, compromising with secular authorities, etc. Still today many seek power for the church through these and other means, like getting the ear of a politician, changing the message to fit the culture, prioritising style over substance, jumping on popular cultural bandwagons, etc. But faithful churches and Christians follow in the steps of the New Testament apostles and their flocks: faithfully preaching God's word and witnessing to the gospel of Jesus Christ in word and deed wherever they go.

3 GOD'S FAMILY

Mark 3:20-35; Matthew 10:32-42

THE BIG IDEA

By joining the church, we join the family in which God is our Father, Jesus our elder brother, and fellow-Christians our brothers and sisters; and we prioritise our love for those in God's family as Jesus did and does.

SUMMARY

Clearly no one told Jesus what most churchgoing believers tend to believe about the family—that they always come first! In Mark 3:20-35, Jesus puts his mother and brothers firmly in a subordinate place when they try to take charge of him; he declares that his family are those who do God's will, clearly implying that his relatives are not doing that right then and cannot have prior claim on him. In Matthew 10:32-42, he announces that all who follow him cannot love their family more than their Saviour and may even find that because they follow Christ, their own relatives become bitter enemies.

This teaching of Jesus may surprise or even shock some people. In child-centred Western culture, where films constantly explore themes to do with the family (or the absence of them), people might easily assume that Christians would automatically put family first. However, this study puts Jesus' countercultural teaching into the wonderful context of God's plan to bring redeemed sinners into one great family, in which he is our Father (Romans 8:15-16), Jesus is our elder brother, and fellow Christians are our brothers and sisters (Romans 8:29).

This teaching challenges those tempted to idolise their earthly family. But knowing that

the church is God's family, and that Jesus identifies so intimately with his brothers and sisters, also brings great comfort to those from a dysfunctional family or whose relatives have become their persecutors. In our world of failing families and isolated individuals, we Christians should also realise how powerfully the church displays the flourishing life that the gospel brings when it is seen as the extended family that in fact it is.

Note: Those from a dysfunctional family might struggle in this study if they focus on their own experience. Instead, encourage them to think about a family that they look up to or the kind of family they have always wished for.

OPTIONAL EXTRA

Get people to talk about a family that they love and/or one that they dislike from a book, film or TV show. The aim is to show that God designed the family to be a wonderful source of security, enjoyment and happiness, but when families go wrong, they cause terrible pain and damage.

GUIDANCE FOR QUESTIONS

1. Mention two people who are important to you and briefly explain their importance: a. A family member ... b. A fellow Christian ... This question aims to get people thinking about fellow Christians as spiritual relatives.

2. In verse 21, why do you think Jesus' family had decided that he was out of his mind? At this point in Jesus' public ministry, his fame had "gone viral" (see

3:7-10). Constantly mobbed by excited crowds, he and his disciples weren't even able to eat (v 20); clearly they were not living a normal life. Meanwhile, Jesus was also attracting the hostility of the religious leaders (e.g. 3:1-6, 22). But despite these difficulties, Jesus didn't withdraw from his work of teaching, healing and training his followers.

• **What did they want to do, and what was their motivation, do you think?** They wanted "to take charge of him"—presumably to make him give up his public ministry for the sake of his health and personal safety. They planned to impose on him what they thought was good for him. Doubtless, they were motivated by concern for his welfare, but good motives don't automatically safeguard us from wrong actions.

3. What evidence in verses 22-27 shows that the family's view of Jesus was totally inappropriate? (Think about what Jesus has been doing and with what power he's been doing it.) Get people to point out (1) what Jesus was doing and (2) how the religious leaders tried to explain this. Then (3) help them work out Jesus' illustration in verse 27. We see (1) Jesus' power to drive out demons and (2) the logical impossibility of this being a satanic power; (3) put these together and we see that Jesus is the stronger man who defeats the strong man: Satan (v 27). In other words, Jesus has the power of God. This is the one that Jesus' family were coming to take charge of!

4. How does Jesus then redefine his family, and what is his purpose in doing that, do you think? He declares that his family comprises anyone who does God's will. He is showing (1) what is most important in being his follower—obedience

to God—and (2) the wonderful result of obeying God, which is to become part of his family, with all the joys and benefits that a true family relationship entails.

• **Read Luke 8:19-21. How do Jesus' words here explain what he means by "whoever does God's will"?** Such people are "those who hear God's word and put it into practice". This parallel account in Luke's Gospel clarifies what it means for us today to do God's will.

5. In Mark 3, compare where Jesus' true family are (v 34) with where his biological family are (v 31-32); then compare what both groups are doing. Jesus looks at those seated around him as he speaks about his true family (v 34). They are inside the house with Jesus, listening to him; and they include those who will put his words into practice. His biological family, however, are outside the house, trying to stop him from teaching.

• **Why does Jesus prioritise the former?** Because of their rejection of Jesus and his mission, he won't let his biological family have the prior claim on his time and attention or the compliance that they expect. Instead, Jesus prioritises those who listen to and follow him. The key characteristic of those privileged to be in Jesus' family is obedience to him.

⮛

(Ask these questions if you think some people don't understand the gospel or fully follow Jesus Christ.)

• **How confident are you that you are part of God's family?** People might be reluctant to describe themselves this way because this teaching is new to them. Or maybe they have never really understood the gospel or acted on it.

- **What evidence would show that you are one of God's children?** The key characteristic highlighted by Jesus is doing God's will = hearing God's word and putting it into practice. This would be a good place to summarise the gospel and explain how to put it into practice.

6. Read 1 Thessalonians 2:6-12. In what ways does Paul view and treat fellow Christians as his family, just as Jesus did? Paul uses family terms throughout his letters to churches and Christians. Here he speaks of himself being both like "a nursing mother" (v 7) and "a father [dealing] with his own children" (v 11), and he calls these Christians "brothers and sisters" (v 9). The comparisons illuminate different ways in which Paul relates to the Thessalonian Christians: he shows tender care and love like that of a nursing mother; he works and serves alongside and on behalf of his brothers and sisters; and he encourages, comforts and urges the Christians, as a good father would do with his children.

EXPLORE MORE

In Exodus [4:19-23] whom does God call "my son"? The nation of Israel, whom he was about to rescue from Egypt.

And how is this developed in Galatians [6:14-16]? Paul speaks here to "the Israel of God"—those who "follow this rule" (v 16), outlined in verses 14-15. "The Israel of God" is no longer the physical nation of Israel. Instead they are those who boast (or put confidence) only in the cross of the Lord Jesus Christ (v 14); and who have become a "new creation" through God's work in them, and not through anything they have, or haven't, done (v 15).

In 2 Samuel [7:11b-14a], whom does God call "my son"? God tells David that a descendant who will reign on his throne for ever will be "my son" (v 14a).

And how is this developed in Hebrews [1:1-5]? The writer clearly states that Jesus (named in 2:9) is the one whom God named "my Son" (v 5).

[From 1 John 3:7-10] What is the link between the children of God and the Son of God? Many people think everyone is a child of God because God has created everyone. In a sense this is true (see Acts 17:27-29); but John divides everyone into children of God or children of the devil. Children of the devil do what is sinful (v 8). However, the Son of God came to destroy the devil's work (v 8), with the result that some people have been born of God and no longer continue to sin (v 9)—that is, they no longer persist in sin unrepentantly and without concern. The work of the Son of God—Jesus' death on the cross—makes it possible for children of the devil to be born again as children of God.

Is everyone a child of God? If not, who is and who isn't? This question checks people's understanding of who can be part of God's family and how.

7. APPLY: If the church is our family, what privileges and responsibilities does that bring? How should this shape our attitudes and actions? Help your group to think of both the privileges we enjoy as a family and the responsibilities we bear. Our church should be the first people we turn to for love and support, and those among whom we can be open and real. We should meet together informally, and not just for services. Our church should be the people to whom we feel most loyal, whom we most care about protecting, helping and encouraging, and for whom we would drop everything in a crisis, just as we would for our own biological family.

- **How could you help your church feel more like a family?** Again, don't let the group simply grumble. Focus on what each person can do to treat others in their church as they would treat their own relatives in a healthy, happy family.

8. If we would follow Jesus, what is to be our priority throughout life (v 32-33)? We must acknowledge Jesus and not disown him before others. To acknowledge him means to openly believe and witness to the truth that he is God's Son, the only Saviour of all people and the Lord of all, who died and rose again as the only means by which anyone can be saved from sin, forgiven and reconciled with God.

9. What will often prevent people from acknowledging Jesus as Lord and Saviour (v 34-36)? Jesus highlights a follower's earthly family as a not infrequent obstacle to be faced in acknowledging him before others. Christians can encounter intense conflict with relatives who don't acknowledge Jesus. He talks of bringing "a sword" and close family members becoming "enemies". Through history and globally today this conflict has led to the martyrdom of many who put Jesus first. Jesus teaches us not to be surprised by this; rather we should expect it.

- **To overcome this, what attitude do we Christians need (v 37-38)?** Jesus is worth more than anything else in life. The idea that family must take second place to our love for Jesus Christ might surprise and even shock many who assume that good Christians always put their family first. However, Jesus is crystal clear: earthly families, though a God-given gift, must not take precedence over God in our affections. Jesus immediately goes on to talk about his followers taking

up their cross and losing their life. The consequences in this life of putting our family in second place behind our love for Christ can be bitter.

- **What does Jesus promise for those who persevere (v 39)?** That we will find our life (v 39)—the true, perfect and eternal life that can only be found in a right relationship with God through Jesus Christ.

⊻

(Do this question if you think people might misinterpret Jesus' teaching as an excuse to neglect their biological family.)
- **Read 1 Timothy 5:3-8 and 16. What are we Christians commanded to do for our families?** We must not neglect to provide for our family, especially those under our roof (v 8). This includes children and grandchildren caring for their elderly relatives (v 4). To do this is "pleasing to God" (v 4), and to fail in this amounts to denying the faith (v 8). The church also has the same family responsibility to care for those without a biological family to rely on (v 16).

10. How important to Jesus are his family of followers, and how does he show his closeness to us (v 40-42)? We are of supreme importance to Jesus: he identifies so closely with his followers that to welcome and serve even "one of these little ones who is [his] disciple" is to welcome and serve him. We see this again in Jesus' words to Saul of Tarsus when he was waging a campaign of persecution against Christians: "I am Jesus, whom you are persecuting," Jesus says (Acts 9:5).

11. APPLY: In what ways have you seen allegiance to family put above

allegiance to Jesus? (Perhaps you yourself have done this.) Allow people to share from their experience. For example:

• Viewing church as competing for time that we could spend with our family, instead of time when our family can enjoy meeting our extended Christian family.

• Making our involvement in church activities fit around our family activities— whether that's sport, kids' clubs, tuition, or visiting family and friends.

• Becoming over-protective of "family time", signalling that only family is family, and that church is not family but "work" or of less importance.

• **What are the consequences for the gospel and our church?** If we treat church as a religious club or a Sundays-only gathering of otherwise unconnected individuals, our church might never be the kind of community that we saw in Acts 2 (see Study 1). The opportunity for our church to display the flourishing life that the gospel brings will be lost.

12. APPLY: How can this study encourage followers of Jesus who have an unbelieving family? Some Christians will no longer feel at home with their earthly family because, as followers of Jesus, they march to the beat of a different drum. Whether believers are ostracised, persistently criticised and ridiculed, threatened, assaulted, thrown out or even have their lives endangered, all should be able to find a true family among God's people: one where their physical, financial, emotional and spiritual needs are met among believers committed to them throughout life. The family that we join when we turn to Jesus Christ should be greater and more wonderful than any we must leave—and it's an eternal family.

4 GOD'S TEMPLE

Ephesians 2:11-22; 2 Corinthians 6:14 – 7:1

THE BIG IDEA

The church is God's people together, built on the foundation of the apostles and prophets, and Jesus our cornerstone; and as God's dwelling in this world, we are to live differently from others.

SUMMARY

In Old Testament Israel the tabernacle/temple was where God chose to meet with his people. Paul teaches that believers in Christ together form the temple of the living God (e.g. 2 Corinthians 6:16). So today God is found among his church, where the good news of Jesus is proclaimed and lived.

As the Jerusalem Temple was built in a way specified by God, the church of Christ must also be built on the right foundation: that of the apostles and prophets (Ephesians 2:20), found in the Old and New Testaments of the Bible. Jesus Christ is the chief cornerstone: the one who united Jews and Gentiles in the first Christian church, and who continues to unite diverse people as they become his followers.

Everything in the Old Testament temple was cleansed and consecrated for use there and was desecrated if used for everyday or unclean purposes. God's people, the church, are consecrated to live for him. In some senses we are to be separate from the world: purified from everything that contaminates and seeking to grow in holiness (2 Corinthians 7:1).

In practice, this means that the lives of God's people should be different from those of unbelievers. We should not be "yoked together" with unbelievers (6:14). And

we must purify ourselves (7:1); churches need to correct and discipline, seeking the repentance and restoration of professing Christians who fail to live as God commands.

OPTIONAL EXTRA

(See question 1, part 2) A general understanding of the Jerusalem Temple is helpful. Hebrews 9:1-10 describes the layout, activities and purpose of the Old Testament tabernacle, on which the temple was closely based. 1 Kings 8 describes the inauguration of the first temple (v 1-13) and dispels misunderstandings about its purpose (v 27-30). Helpful plans, diagrams, images and video animations of the temple and its furniture can be found online.

GUIDANCE FOR QUESTIONS

1. Where do people today expect to find God? How near to or far from the truth would you say these ideas were? Popular answers include: in beautiful places (e.g. gardens); in so-called holy places (e.g. shrines); in church (check what this means: a building and the atmosphere it evokes?). It's true that we receive a partial revelation of God in creation (Romans 1:20), but the New Testament gives us only two counterparts of the Old Testament temple in the gospel age: Jesus (John 2:19-22) and the church.

• **What do you know about the Jerusalem Temple?** Before Jesus, the Jerusalem Temple was the only place where people could in some sense approach God and receive forgiveness, teaching and blessing. It was located in Israel and embedded in Jewish faith and culture, but Gentiles, by joining the nation of Israel, could also access the blessings of the temple. Similarly today it is only through Jesus Christ and by joining his church that people can truly find God.

EXPLORE MORE [Psalm 27:1-6]
Find three ways in which the temple/ house/tent of the Lord was significant for David ...
- **v 4:** It was where he could gaze on the beauty of the Lᴏʀᴅ and seek him—words which convey a sense of enjoyment in and a relationship with God.
- **v 5:** It was where he could find safety and shelter from his enemies and be raised above them.
- **v 6:** It was where he could joyfully offer sacrifices to God.

In the New Testament the church is described as the temple of God. In what ways does church enable people to find God and enjoy being with him, be kept safe from our enemies, and offer sacrifices to him?
- Through the preaching of the good news of Jesus, people are reconciled to God and grow as his children, learning to trust their loving heavenly Father.
- Through the teaching of God's word, God's people grow in understanding the lies and strategies of God's enemy and the truth of Jesus' victory over all the powers of darkness.
- Only Jesus can offer a sacrifice of atonement (Hebrews 10:12, 14), but by testifying about Christ and living lives worthy of him, Christians offer pleasing sacrifices to God (Hebrews 13:15-16).

2. What do you think is meant by "the foundation of the apostles and prophets" (v 20)? (Your group may find a comparison with 2 Peter 1:16-21 helpful.) Apostles and prophets both taught God's word. "Prophets" equates to the Old Testament Scriptures, the gospel "promised beforehand through [God's] prophets in the Holy Scriptures" (Romans 1:2). "Apostles" is shorthand for the New Testament. The first church "devoted themselves to the apostles' teaching" (Acts 2:42), which showed how Jesus fulfilled the Old Testament promises. So, "the foundation of the apostles and the prophets" means God's word: the Bible.

3. Reread verses 14-18. How has Jesus fulfilled the function of the chief cornerstone in his church? As the chief cornerstone unites two walls, so Jesus has united Jewish and Gentile believers, by reconciling them to God in the same way: through the cross (v 16). Through Jesus, believers of both backgrounds equally have access to the Father by the Spirit (v 18); and from these two previously hostile groups one new and united humanity has been made (v 15): the church.

4. Find three things that verse 21 tells us about all Christian believers. If people are struggling, draw their attention to the verbs ("joined", "rises", "become").
(1) We are "joined together". If Jewish and Gentile difference could be overcome, so can any other ethnic or social division. Believers from all backgrounds are to be joined together, as stones are cemented together to make a building.
(2) We are to "rise" to become the building that God has planned us to be, changing, growing and developing in unity and purpose.
(3) We are to "become a holy temple in the Lord". "Holy" means consecrated for God's use. The tabernacle/temple furniture and utensils were set apart for use only there (Exodus 30:22-29). To be holy means being cleansed from anything that makes us

unacceptable to God, and dedicated to his purposes, not living for the things everyone else lives for.

5. What are the implications of verse 22? Think about...

- **our privilege (see 1 Kings 8:27-29 and 9:3):** Old Testament people of faith knew that God cannot be confined to one building (1 Kings 8:27); but he chose to reveal his presence in the Jerusalem Temple (e.g. 1 Kings 8:10-11). There people received atonement for sin through sacrifices; they looked to the temple for assurance that their prayers would be heard (1 Kings 8:29; 9:3); and there they celebrated God's goodness. God now chooses to reveal his presence in the church, where we learn of and trust in Christ's atonement for sin, in whom we have assurance that God hears our prayers; and as church we celebrate God's goodness together.

- **our mission (see 1 Kings 8:41-43):** The temple was where even someone from outside Israel could find God. Today people find God through the church's proclamation of the gospel.

6. APPLY: What part can we play in ensuring that our church...

- **is "built on the foundation of the apostles and prophets"?** Without the correct foundations, a building won't stand for long.
  - Faithful Bible teaching must be at the centre of the leadership and ministry of our church.
  - We need to be fed by God's word in church and in our own Bible reading, and to help others listen and grow from God's word. We can reflect this priority in the conversations we have with one another.

- Every believer, to a greater or lesser extent, can learn Scripture well enough to spot when a leader or fellow believer is drifting from the foundations, and to challenge that where necessary.

- **is "joined together" in Jesus our cornerstone?** The key is to focus on what unites us. All are reconciled to God through the cross, so we all share what is most important in life and eternity. All differences, then, must be secondary. When our differences cause division, we must remember the gospel and that we are both part of the one new humanity created by Jesus—and we must treat each other accordingly.

7. How does Paul contrast believers and unbelievers? Complete the table.
There is a complete polarity between believers in Christ and unbelievers; the two cannot be mixed. But it's important to understand that what is true of believers here is only because of God's grace in our lives.

VERSE	BELIEVERS	UNBELIEVERS
14	Righteousness	Wickedness
14	Light	Darkness
15	Christ	Belial
16	The temple of God	Idols

8. "Do not be yoked together with unbelievers." Does Paul's instruction here mean believers should have no contact whatever with unbelievers? (See 1 Corinthians 5:9-10.)
Paul doesn't prohibit believers from associating with unbelievers, since, he says, "in that case you would have to leave this world" (v 10). The picture

of the yoke is key: binding two animals together so they have to go the same way. (*Note:* Unequal yoking of animals was prohibited in the law, Deuteronomy 22:10.)

- **What kind of partnerships does Paul have in mind, do you think?** Those where a believer and unbeliever are equals together in the same enterprise, in which the unbeliever can influence the enterprise as much as the believer; e.g. a romantic relationship tending toward marriage; a Christian ministry team; equal-partner business arrangements; significant friendships (see also Psalm 1:1).

9. Since we are "the temple of the living God", what four things must we do (three in 6:17 and one in 7:1)? And what will each look like?
(1) "Come out from them" (6:17): Paul quotes Isaiah 52:11. Isaiah has prophesied God's liberation of the Jews from Babylon and now calls them to leave exile; Babylon is no longer where they are to live so they should start the journey home. Applied to Christians, this calls us to turn from making life in this world our priority,, and focus instead on eternity (Colossians 3:1-2).
(2) "Be separate" (v 17): Or, as Isaiah says, speaking to those who would carry the temple articles back to Jerusalem, "Be pure" (Isaiah 52:11). Christians are to be different from the rest of the world because of our purity of life and behaviour.
(3) "Touch no unclean thing" (v 17): Under the Law of Moses, if someone who was consecrated to work in the temple touched something unclean, they had to be purified from uncleanness before they could take up their responsibilities again (e.g. Leviticus 22:1-9). Similarly, Christians contaminated by participation in unclean, immoral or ungodly things become disqualified from Christian witness and mission. (See next point.)

(4) "Purify ourselves from everything that contaminates body and spirit" (7:1). 1 John 1:7 is helpful: if we walk in the light with Jesus and in fellowship with other believers, the blood of Jesus purifies us. Notice that the work of purification is done by Jesus; our part is to stay close to Jesus and his people.

- **What promises are we given that spur us to do these things (v 16, 18)?** *Verse 16:* God promises his presence among his people and assures us that we belong to him. This is the heart of what it means for the church to be the temple of the living God. *Verse 18:* God will bring us into his family. Those struggling with the cost of ending unequally yoked relationships need to hear the tenderness and intimacy of these promises from God himself.

10. In practice, what does it look like for a church to purify themselves? The New Testament teaches how the church should treat brothers and sisters who are not living as God has commanded. You could divide your group into pairs, and assign each one of the following passages:
Matthew 18:15-17: Jesus gives a clear procedure to follow when a brother or sister sins. First, we who spot the sin should speak privately to rebuke and correct; if this is rejected, involve one or two other believers as witnesses. If this is rejected, bring the matter before the whole church. If this is rejected, the church should treat the person as an unbeliever.
Galatians 6:1: If a believer is caught in a sin, we should seek to restore them gently, always conscious of our own vulnerability to sin.
2 Thessalonians 3:6, 14-15: Keep away from any believer who persistently refuses to live according to the teaching of Scripture (the context is refusing to work), so that they will feel ashamed. But don't treat them

as an enemy; rather, warn them as a fellow believer.

1 Corinthians 5:12-13: "Expel the wicked person from among you." (The context is a believer acting in gross immorality which would shock even pagans, v 1.) Such a person can no longer be part of the church or receive assurance that they are saved from sin. Instead, treat them as an unbeliever. The aim is to bring them to repentance so they can be restored to the church family, but if that doesn't happen, the church will be kept pure: our witness will not be compromised nor our people corrupted.

11. APPLY: Discuss a lifelike situation in which a believer is yoked together with an unbeliever. How might you and your church need to respond? Allow the group to choose the situation: romantic relationship, ministry, equal-partnership business or significant friendship. Hopefully, the discussion will touch on the points raised in question 10. Help your group to be constructive in their discussion; e.g. take a moment to pray for fearless Scriptural wisdom among your leaders in such a situation. *Note:* If any members of your group are married to non-believers this discussion will need to be handled with particular love and care.

12. APPLY: Why is it so difficult for us to keep the church of Christ pure? Reasons include the following:

- Our individualistic, anti-authoritarian society makes it difficult for us to speak to people on these issues, or to hear rebuke and correction.
- We fear offending and losing church members more than we fear not heeding these commands.
- We're aware of our own failings, so we

think we're disqualified from rebuking and correcting others. Instead we should be spurred to show gentleness and compassion.

- We've lost sight of the bigger picture—the need in our community for a countercultural family of Christ's people who display by purity of life the power and attractiveness of the gospel.

- **What are some of the potential consequences if we fail to purify ourselves as a church?**
  - Corruption—other church members will be tempted to go along with the world rather than following Christ as distinctively holy people.
  - Our gospel witness will be compromised—if Christ's followers look and act like everyone else in our society, why would anyone follow him at cost to themselves?
  - Our church might no longer be "the temple of the living God"—since we will have given up revering God by perfecting holiness among ourselves (7:1). In the end our church might no longer be a true church of Jesus Christ.

5 1 Corinthians 12; Ephesians 4:1-7, 11-16
CHRIST'S BODY

THE BIG IDEA

Christ's church makes up his body: we enjoy diversity in unity, and together we are to grow up into maturity to become a body that fits our head, Jesus.

SUMMARY

Paul's image in 1 Corinthians 12—of God's people as a body with Christ as our head—is a very effective picture of what the church is universally and should be locally. God's people are all different, each with different gifts of the Spirit, and yet all are united in Christ, through the same Spirit. This unity in diversity is unique to the church of Christ— different from both individualism, which destroys community, and uniformity, which destroys individuality.

Paul draws very practical lessons from the body image. No Christian should withdraw from the church because they feel they don't belong; and no Christian should exclude another believer because they are different and thought of as weak or unpresentable in some way. Individually, we need to trust that God has gifted us to play a necessary part in his church; and also that he is using for the common good those who, we think, have little to offer. Importantly, the Spirit doesn't give us gifts for our own personal fulfilment but for the common good—and that's only achieved by serving others with those gifts.

Paul also talks of the church as a body in Ephesians 4, where we see again diversity and unity, and the purpose of Christ's gifts: teaching to equip God's people and, when equipped, serving. Together the gifts build up the body of Christ, which grows in maturity as we become more like Jesus.

OPTIONAL EXTRA

Give everyone a pencil and sheet of paper folded vertically into three sections. Everyone draws on the left-hand section the head of an animal of their choice looking to the left, with the top and bottom lines ending just over the fold on the middle section; then fold the left-hand section to the back. Everyone passes their paper to the person on their right, who, without looking at the head, draws on the middle section the body and front legs of an animal looking to the left, starting where the outline of the head ends. Repeat the process, with the next person drawing the back legs and a tail on the third section. Then unfold the pieces of paper to reveal some mighty strange animals! (Links with question 11, about how the body needs to be suitable for its head.)

GUIDANCE FOR QUESTIONS

1. In what ways is your church a diverse group of people? As we'll see, diverse unity is a key characteristic of a healthy church. This question might encourage your group, as they see that God is at work in diverse people; or it may be challenging if everyone in your church is similar.

- **In what ways is your church a united group of people?** Note the reasons given for unity in your church. Is it because everyone is similar? That's uniformity rather than the unity we're about to see.

2. Look at verses 4-14. What type of differences within a church does Paul highlight in verses 4-6? What (or rather, who) is the reason behind this diversity? The Spirit distributes different kinds of gifts, service and working in Christians (v 4-6; see v 8-10 and v 28-30). Other lists elsewhere (e.g. Romans 12:6-8), show that no list is comprehensive. Just as the body is not made up of only one part (1 Corinthians 12:14), so Christians should not expect to all receive the same gifts of the Spirit. He is the reason behind this wonderful diversity.

• **What reason does Paul give for the unity of God's people?** Only one Spirit distributes all the gifts to the different Christians, so in every believer it is the same God at work (v 6). All Christians are baptised by the one Spirit and given the one Spirit to drink (v 13). Just as different body parts make one body, so in the Spirit diverse Christians have a deep, enduring unity (v 12).

3. What is the purpose for which the Spirit gives God's people various gifts (v 7)? "The common good." So we are to use our gifts to do good to God's people. Our gifts are identified by our contribution to that common good and not by how fulfilled something makes us feel.

• **What can go wrong if we forget this purpose?** We'll focus on how we feel and what we like. It's possible to have a passion to do something for which we are not gifted by the Spirit; e.g. an intense desire to sing upfront in church or a burning ambition to be a Bible teacher. But a Spirit-given gift must contribute to the common good—building the church (in maturity and numbers). Perhaps your singing or Bible teaching doesn't do this— because you have no ability, or because your character undermines that attempted ministry, or because the church has plenty of singers and Bible teachers, and needs creche helpers and youth workers instead. In those cases, however fulfilled you feel in

singing or Bible teaching, you don't have that Spirit-given gift.

4. What are the implications of the fact that Christ's church is like a body for when…
• **you feel different to everyone else (v 15-20)?** Just because you are different from others in your church, it doesn't mean that you are not part of the church. You shouldn't for that reason withdraw but rather trust that God has placed you there, like an essential body part, for the good of that church (v 18).

• **someone else is different to you (v 21-26)?** Just because someone is somehow different to everyone else in your church, it doesn't mean that you can reject them (often done implicitly by avoidance, cliques, etc.). Paul mentions people whom others view as weaker or less honourable than themselves, or even find unpresentable (v 22-23)—people we react to with embarrassment, frustration or even disgust.

5. What kind of people might Paul have in mind when he mentions those who "seem to be weaker" (v 22), or that "we think are less honourable", or are "unpresentable" (v 23)? Paul's society, like all societies, suffered from various divisions. Jews and Gentiles despised one another and had very different notions of honour. Slaves and free men took different paths through life, as did men and women. There were the unskilled and uneducated, beggars, criminals, social outcasts and those who were chronically sick or disabled. In church some gifts were viewed more highly than others, and those with "wrong" gifts were probably despised.

• **How does Paul view such people in**

the body of Christ (v 22-23)? Such people only "*seem* to be weaker" (v 22) and "we *think* [they] are less honourable" (v 23). In fact, they are "indispensable" (v 22; see question 12.)

• **What clues does the passage give about how we should treat such people?** Paul tells us to give "special treatment" to those who are "unpresentable" (v 23-24) and so reflect the character of God, who gives "greater honour" to those who lack it (v 24). The goal is that all parts of the body should have equal concern for each other (v 25). In society, many factors contribute to people's differing levels of status. But there is only one status within the church: we are all forgiven sinners, loved children of God, witnesses of Jesus Christ and recipients of the Holy Spirit. But to show this equality, we need to give particular help and honour to believers who are marginalised or despised in society, making special efforts to include them and show their importance to us. Paul's language of modesty (v 23) implies "covering" what makes some unpresentable—not drawing attention to deficiencies but "clothing" them with gospel truth (e.g. Rod is not an ex-drug addict but a precious Christian brother with a wonderful story of how Jesus has changed him).

6. Look at verses 27-31. What are "the greater gifts"?

Paul orders the first three gifts only—apostles, prophets and teachers—suggesting that these are the greater gifts he speaks of. All three involve communicating God's word. In 14:1-3 we see Paul's priority for the gathered church: people strengthened, encouraged and comforted by hearing God's word, communicated through those who are gifted to do so. **Why are they called that, do you think?** Remember (from Session 4) that the church is built on the foundation of the apostles and prophets: the Bible. So without these gifts, there can be no church. That's not to say that other gifts are unimportant. They are needed to bring people to hear the word, or to confirm the truth and power of God's word.

7. APPLY: From this passage, how would you try to help...

You might prefer to choose just one scenario or distribute them to pairs or triplets.

• **someone who is convinced that God has called them to be a Bible teacher?** Are they already teaching the Bible in some way? If yes, is that contributing to the common good? Do people listen and understand? Are their hearers encouraged or challenged to be more godly and to trust in Christ more? If yes, then great! If not, ask why this person thinks they have a gift of Bible teaching. Does their answer agree with what we have learned?

• **someone who is upset that they haven't been chosen for the "worship-leader" rota, insisting that this is their special gift?** Remember, if this is a gift of the Spirit, it will benefit the common good. Singing ability is not the only consideration. And ironically, an attitude that insists on exercising this "gift", regardless of what most helps the common good, itself undermines it. Such a "gift" is merely a natural talent when it lacks this defining characteristic of a gift of the Spirit.

• **someone who believes they have nothing to contribute in church?** That's impossible! Paul triple-underlines this by imagining a foot, an eye and an ear all wrongly concluding that they don't belong to the body because they are not, respectively, a hand, an ear or a nose! Notice that these parts already belong to the body, regardless of how they feel about themselves. Not even thinking you don't belong stops you belonging to the body. And if you belong, you have a contribution to make. This person needs help to see how they can contribute to the common good of God's people.

- **someone who is embarrassed to be paired with an elderly woman on the church welcome team?** This sister might be considered weak or unpresentable but this person should know that this elderly sister is in fact indispensable to their church, regardless of however cool, cutting-edge and on-trend they would like their church to appear.

8. APPLY: What kind of people might be viewed as weak, less honourable or unpresentable in your church? (*Note:* Don't discuss specific individuals—which risks disregarding what Paul says (v 23) about treating such people with special honour and modesty.) Think about what could put someone into the weak/dishonourable/unpresentable category in your church. Culture or class? Education? Occupation? Family background? Personality? Disabilities? Learning difficulties? A sinful past?

- **What would it look like to treat people from these categories with special honour?** Some ideas to get the discussion going: What might they uniquely contribute to the common good? What ministry or team could they be part of? What hospitality or fellowship could you extend? How could they testify about what Jesus has done for them? What can other believers learn from them? How can other Christians serve and encourage them?

9. *Unity* (verses 1-6): How has God produced unity in the body of Christ? Through the Spirit, who unites all who are in Christ—"the unity of the Spirit" (v 3)—into "one body", not many. This is true of all God's people throughout history and worldwide—despite diverse church groups, denominations and practices. So it should also be true of saved people within a local church. The evidence of this unity is that all believers in Jesus share the same fundamental things: we have one Lord only, we follow one faith that does not change with time or culture, we undergo one baptism—in the name of the Father, Son and Holy Spirit (Matthew 28:19), regardless of precisely how it's done in practice— and we worship the same God, the one who has revealed himself in Scripture (Ephesians 4:5-6).

- **What responsibility regarding our unity is given to believers in the body of Christ?** Verse 3: We're to "*make every effort to keep* the unity of the Spirit" (my emphasis). Unity has already been given to us by God. All that is required now is that we work to preserve it rather than undermine it. Verse 2 gives practical instructions for this: through humility, gentleness, patience and love.

10. *Diversity* (verses 11-12): Two tasks are mentioned for which Christ apportions grace (v 7) to all believers.
- **What is the task of those given the gifts described in verse 11?** These people are gifted to communicate God's word. Scripture thoroughly equips God's servants "for every good work" (2 Timothy 3:16-17), so these gifts are given to *equip* God's people.

- **What is the task of all the other believers (v 12)?** Equipped by God's word "for works of service", they are to serve God and others.

• **What is the one purpose that all work towards (end of v 12)?** To build up the church. Given what follows, Paul must mean building up the church in maturity, but the mention of evangelists suggests that increased numbers are also in view.

11. *Maturity* **(verses 13-16). Maturity among God' people means becoming increasingly like Jesus Christ—"attaining to the whole measure of the fullness of Christ" (v 13) and becoming "in every respect the mature body of him who is the head, that is, Christ" (v 15). What does it look like when we are mature...**

• **in our faith (v 13-14)?** Unity in the faith and knowledge of God's Son. This knowledge also becomes the benchmark against which we test all teaching. We don't agree with everybody; rather we discern truth and error, and that anchors us.

• **in our relationships with fellow believers (v 15)?** We speak "the truth in love" to one another—a rare combination. Often we only do one or the other. But truth and love are equally seen among mature believers. (If you did the Optional Extra activity above, refer back to it here. The idea is that the body needs to fit with its head.)

• **in our commitment to our church (v 16)?** Each person is at work, equipping or serving to join, support and build up the church in love.

EXPLORE MORE [Psalm 133]
Where does the oil flow from and to? How does this relate to what we've seen in Ephesians 4:15? From the head down to the body of Aaron, just as our unity

flows from Christ by his Spirit.
Why is oil such a good picture of unity? (see Psalm 23:5; 45:7; 104:15)? Oil is associated with good living and joy, and this is how unity affects God's people.
What does [the miracle of dew from Mount Hermon falling on Mount Zion] tell us about unity? Unity in the church is produced by the supernatural work of the Spirit in believers—it is a miracle! This world can produce stifling uniformity but not the delightful unity-in-diversity of the mature church. Only Christ by his Spirit can produce that.
Think about your experiences of the unity of God's people. How do they match the truths expressed in this psalm?

12. APPLY: **How do "those parts of the body that seem to be weaker" (1 Corinthians 12:22) help the whole body to increasingly mature in Christ-likeness?** If we're to attain to the measure of Christ and grow to be the mature body of our head, we need to develop his characteristics: humble servant-heartedness, love for the weak and outcasts, etc. When we love and serve brothers and sisters who seem weak, dishonourable or unpresentable, we exercise character "muscles" that otherwise never get used, and we grow the character of Jesus.

• **What could this look like in practice in your church?** Some ideas: the rich helping the poor; the wise and knowledgeable helping the ignorant and simple; families helping the isolated; the healthy and strong helping the sick and the weak; the child-free helping those with childcare responsibilities, and so on.

6 Ephesians 5:25-32; 2 Corinthians 11:1-5, 13-15
CHRIST'S BRIDE

THE BIG IDEA

As the model of the husband in Christian marriage, Jesus loves the church: giving up his life for us, cleansing us, making us holy and working to present us as his beautiful bride—when finally, holy and blameless, we will live wedded to him for ever in the new creation.

SUMMARY

Hearing Christ described as the Bridegroom and the church as his bride, we might think that the relationship between the church and our Lord is modelled on human marriage, but in Ephesians 5 Paul shows that human marriage should be modelled on the true marriage of Christ and his people, which will take place in the new creation.

Paul shows Christ, the ultimate Husband, giving himself up for the church when he suffered death on the cross to atone for our sins (v 25). He has both already made his people holy by the washing of his word (the message of the gospel) (v 26) and continues to do so, as he works towards his goal of one day presenting to himself a radiant, holy and blameless church (v 27). And he models a husband's love in the way he constantly cares for his people (v 29).

In 2 Corinthians 11, Paul likens his own ministry to the role of a marriage broker, with the goal of presenting the Corinthian Christians as a virgin bride to Christ, the husband they have been promised to in marriage. Paul is concerned that they could be enticed away from their sincere and pure devotion to Christ by false and deceiving teachers: "super-apostles" who look impressive but who teach a Jesus, a Spirit

and a gospel that is very different from the apostles' message.

The depiction of Christ and his people as Bridegroom and bride and the return of Christ as the wedding day of the Lamb (Revelation 19:6-8) highlights the thrilling future and assured "happily-ever-after" ending that lies in store for the people of God. This view of the church can powerfully strengthen us to faithfully endure in this world. The challenges here for God's people are to be thankful for all that our Bridegroom has done and is doing for his bride, and to encourage each other to persevere in sincere and pure devotion to him.

OPTIONAL EXTRA

(Extends question 1; or you could do this activity before answering question 5.) Talk about weddings that you have been to. Share stories of the most spectacular, the funniest, the strangest and the most moving. Discuss why weddings are still such major celebrations despite the continuing long-term trend to undermine marriage in our society. (Why isn't a couple's decision to co-habit celebrated in the same way as a wedding celebrates a marriage?)

GUIDANCE FOR QUESTIONS

1. Think of some films, books, TV dramas or stage shows which end with a marriage. How do those kind of endings make you feel—jubilant or cynical? Why, do you think? Some people will love the idea of a story ending with two people getting happily married. Note that humans universally long for the hope of a "happy-ever-after" because it is something God created us for, and that we all could have enjoyed if human rebellion against God had not earned the consequences of fallenness in this world (see Genesis 3). Others will feel dissatisfied with this kind of happy ending, suspecting that it is an impossible fantasy and preferring a more realistic outcome. People's preferences could be affected by their own experiences of marriage.

2. What or who is the original model in this passage, and what or who is the copy? Christ and the church is the "original", of which human marriage is a "copy". In verse 32 Paul reveals that when he describes marriage as it was intended to be, he is in fact describing the relationship between Christ and the church. The "mystery" of marriage is something that until then had been hidden but was finally being revealed through the message of Jesus Christ. John Piper says of verse 32, "Marriage is a mystery. There is more here than meets the eye … I think it's this: God didn't create the union of Christ and the church after the pattern of human marriage; just the reverse, he created human marriage on the pattern of Christ's relation to the church" ("Marriage: A Matrix of Christian Hedonism", https://www.desiringgod.org/messages/marriage [Oct. 16 1983], accessed 23/6/20).

3. List the things that Christ has done (past) for his bride, the church (v 25-26).
• He has loved the church and gave himself up for her; this refers to his atoning death on the cross.
• He has made the church holy and has cleansed us through his word, which "washes" us like water cleaning the body. This is past when referring to the point at

which we were born again, as Peter says, "through the living and enduring word of God" (1 Peter 1:23). John tells us that when someone is born of God, "they cannot go on sinning" (1 John 3:9).
• **For what purpose (v 27)?** Jesus' goal is "to present [believers together] to himself as a radiant church, without stain or wrinkle or any other blemish", which in actuality means that we will be "holy and blameless".

4. List the things that Christ is doing now (present) for his bride, the church (v 26, 29). *Verse 26:* Making us holy by cleansing us through the "washing" action of God's word is also present: Christ is doing this in the church right now. Hebrews 4:12 tells us that "the word of God is alive and active". Paul could say to the Thessalonian Christians that God's word was "at work" in them (1 Thessalonians 2:13). *Verse 29:* Christ feeds and cares for the church as his own body. This too refers to Christ's work in us through his word; as we've seen, Christ gives teaching gifts to his church to equip his people to build up the body (Ephesians 4:11-13).

• **What words here describe the kind of church that Christ will produce?** Loved, holy, cleansed, radiant, without stain or wrinkle or any other blemish, blameless, fed, cared for. Perhaps spend a moment giving thanks to God.

EXPLORE MORE [Isaiah 54:1-8]
What has this "wife" suffered in her previous experience of "marriage" with another "husband"? v 1: Barrenness/infertility—a cause of desolation (v 1) for those who suffered it in Old Testament Israel. **v 4 (see also v 6):** Shame in her youth, probably because of desertion

and rejection by her husband. **v 4 again:** Widowhood—without husbands or grown sons to protect and provide for them, widows were among the most vulnerable people in society.

The woman representing Israel is no longer in a marriage where she is sinned against; she is now the wife of her Maker. But how do we know that in this utterly different and incomparably better marriage, she herself has sinned (v 7-8)? God abandoned her (v 7) in a surge of anger (v 8), showing that this time round she was guilty of wrong in taking the path that led to her shame and suffering.

What could she have been guilty of? God's first response to her sounds very much like a husband's jealousy because of his wife's adultery. For instance, notice that he intends to call and bring her *back* (v 6, 7). Clearly, she has strayed from him.

How is God's graciousness seen in Isaiah 54, in the face of this adultery/idolatry? It is God's compassion that is most emphasised here: he chooses to treat Israel, his wife, as someone shamed through ill-treatment rather than because of her sin (v 6); he abandoned her "for a brief moment" (v 7), but he will show her "everlasting kindness" (v 8). This is a "wife" with a tarnished history and reputation, but "the God of all the earth" (v 5) is determined to show her "deep compassion" (v 7).

Looking again at those verses, what will our future be like? It will be marked by joy (v 1); fruitfulness, pictured as descendants, and prosperity, pictured as settling in cities (v 2-3); no more fear, shame, disgrace, or reproach (v 4); no more distress or rejection (v 6); no more abandonment by God (v 7); living face to face with God in a relationship of everlasting kindness (v 8)—and all because of his compassionate grace. This is the ultimate "happily-ever-after" conclusion,

but unlike the cheesy closing scenes of many films, this ending will be real for all who are part of the bride of Christ.

5. APPLY: God's people collectively are the bride of Christ. How will this change the way you view church? Properly understood, this image of God's people will transform our view of church. No longer can we view it, as people so often do, just as…

- a religious club for preserving Christian heritage, defending morality or doing good in society.
- a group of aged, odd or nice but out-of-touch people.
- a spent force in slow decline.

Instead we understand that the future for God's people is more wonderful than we can dream of, our security in Christ's love now is unfailing, and the importance of Christ's church is unequalled by anything else in this world.

- **How will it better motivate you to live for Jesus Christ?** Even today, nothing speaks more eloquently of love than a wedding. And in the marriage of Christ to his people, we see the ultimate wedding expressing the ultimate love. The greatest motivation to live for Christ is knowing the love of God for us. As John says, "We love because he first loved us" (1 John 4:19).

6. What is Paul's goal for the Corinthian Christians (v 2)? To present them to Christ, their husband, as "a pure virgin".

- **What does it mean in practice to be a "pure virgin" here (v 3)?** To continue in "sincere and pure devotion to Christ". Spend a few minutes talking about what "sincere" and "pure" mean. ("Sincere" devotion is free from pretence, deception and hypocrisy; "pure" devotion is not mixed with devotion to other things.)

7. Who could derail Paul's objective, and how could they do that?

• **v 3:** Satan—the snake—by deceiving God's people so that their minds are led astray from sincere and pure devotion to Christ.

• **v 4:** People who come among God's people and preach a different Jesus, a different Spirit and a different gospel from that which the Corinthian Christians have already received from the apostles.

• **v 5:** So-called "super-apostles"—who set themselves up as superior to Christ's apostles.

Note: It might be helpful to point out that the apostles were those who saw the risen Christ and were commissioned by him to lead his church and oversee the development of the New Testament. But the warnings here apply equally to the false teachers that the church continues to encounter today—those who do not uphold the apostles' teaching as it is preserved for us in the Bible.

8. How precisely can false teachers deceive us (v 13-15)? They masquerade as apostles of Christ and servants of righteousness. In other words they look good; they look like Christian leaders and good-living people.

• **What are the implications of this?** We should beware of being impressed by appearances alone. We need to listen to a teacher's message also.

9. How can we spot false teachers (v 5-11)? By comparing them with the real thing. For instance, look at Paul's "boasting" (v 10); it's all about things that the super-apostles would never boast about: his knowledge of the gospel (v 6), which was the first message that these Christians received (v 4), rather than any skill in public speaking; and his self-sacrifice for these Christians—especially financial sacrifices— which shows them how he loves them.

• **How can we avoid being taken in?** To avoid being taken in by deceiving appearances, we must compare any taught message with the gospel passed down to us from Christ's apostles; and we should look for evidence of loving self-sacrifice, including willingness to suffer loss financially, in our church leaders.

10. APPLY: What might it look like to support the ongoing work in your church of presenting Christ's people as a pure virgin to their husband? Share and discuss practical ideas for helping one another to continue in sincere (unhypocritical) and pure (unmixed) devotion to Christ. We will all need to remember what the apostolic message of Christ is and what true Christ-like love looks like so that we can be alert to those who would deceive God's people and entice them away from Christ.

7 Ephesians 2:1-10; 3:2-11
GOD'S MASTERPIECE

THE BIG IDEA

God's purpose for Christ's church involves Christians in the greatest cosmic story ever. As God's handiwork, created in Christ to do good works, we reveal God's grace to every future age; and in our Christ-centred unity with all believers, we display to the heavenly realms God's multi-coloured wisdom.

SUMMARY

This session deals with an aspect of New Testament teaching about the church that some might not have heard of before. Hopefully they will feel amazement, thrill and wonder. In Ephesians, Paul portrays Christ's church, first, as the clearest revelation of God's grace for all ages to come (chapter 2) and, second, as the fulfilment of God's promises, seen in his power to bring about something previously unimaginable by uniting Gentiles and Israelites in Christ, for the purpose of displaying his wisdom to all heavenly powers (chapter 3).

In 2:1-10 Paul describes the helpless and hopeless alienation of unsaved people from God and all his blessings. He depicts sinners as dead in transgressions, enslaved to the world and the evil one, disobedient to God and deserving only of his wrath. He contrasts this profoundly abject state with the love, mercy, kindness and grace of God in doing for his people everything that we cannot. And then he reveals God's purpose in all this: as God's handiwork, created in Christ to do good works, Christians will reveal now and in the future the incomparable riches of God's grace. We are part of a "bigger story" that brings wonderful and enduring enlightenment to the world.

In 3:2-11 Paul shares a further phenomenal God-given insight into God's purpose for Christ's church when he talks of a mystery now revealed to the apostles—something previously not understood even by God's people but now made clear. The mystery is that believers of Jewish and of Gentile origin alike *both* receive through Christ everything that God has promised, and so in him they are united into one body. (If we don't know about the entrenched hostility that historically existed between Jewish and Gentile people, this revealed mystery might not seem as astounding to us as it did then.) But Paul has more to say: God's purpose in uniting in Christ's church such disparate and mutually hostile people is to make known his multi-coloured wisdom to all rulers and authorities in the heavenly realms. The church's significance extends far beyond this world.

As we seek to do the good works that God has prepared for us to do, and as we make every effort to keep the unity of the Spirit among the people of God, God is using us to further his awe-inspiring purposes for the church. In this way, we live as part of the greatest and most enduring "bigger story" ever. We can be encouraged to know that Christ's church—which we often experience as unimpressive, deeply imperfect, powerless and reviled—has eternal cosmic significance. Truly it can be called God's masterpiece.

OPTIONAL EXTRA

Work through this list of famous mysteries and ask people to vote on whether they think each has been solved or not: (1)

Where was Richard III buried after dying in battle? (2) Who was Jack the Ripper? (3) What happened to the Franklin Arctic expedition of 1845? (4) What caused the Tunguska blast of 1908? (5) Did Irving and Mallory reach the top of Everest in 1924? (6) What happened to the crew of the Mary Celeste? (7) What happened to aviator Amelia Earhart? (8) Did the Grand Duchess Anastasia, daughter of the last Russian tsar, survive when her family was executed by the Bolsheviks? Numbers 1, 3, 4, and 8 have been solved at the time of writing. These are akin to the biblical definition of a "mystery": something not understood in the past but now revealed. Paul mentions this kind of mystery in Ephesians 3:3 and 6 (see question 7).

Alternatively, share stories of how unity in Christ brought together people who otherwise would have been bitter enemies (see questions 7-9).

GUIDANCE FOR QUESTIONS

1. What are the big "stories" or causes, if any, that people seek to live for— things that are bigger and will last longer than themselves? Many people don't live for anything bigger than their immediate family, home, business or hobbies. But "bigger stories" might include political parties or movements, charities or relief initiatives, national or cultural pride, human rights, music, technological progress, scientific discovery, geographical exploration, historical research, art or music or literature, and so on.

- **What kinds of things limit the grandeur of these "bigger stories"?**
Changing social conditions, cultural values and human nature mean that as time goes by these stories lose relevance, get forgotten, undergo revision or fall into disrepute, or are covered up or destroyed.

Ultimately, everything on earth created by humans is destined to perish; nothing will last for ever.

2. List all the things in verses 1-3 that Christians ("you") did or were. We were dead in transgressions and sins (v 1); we followed the ways of the world and the evil one, and so we were disobedient (v 2); we lived like everyone else in this world doing what our sinful nature wanted and thought (v 3); we deserved God's wrath (v 3).

- **"You were *dead* in your transgressions and sins, in which you used to *live*" (v 1-2). What does Paul mean by "dead", and what are the implications of this?**
Paul here describes how everyone without Christ, though living in this world, is as helpless, hopeless and beyond human intervention as a corpse. Just as a corpse has no power to do anything, unbelievers have no power, specifically to stop sinning. Just as a corpse cannot offer a relationship with anyone or benefit from one, so unbelievers have no relationship with God. Just as a corpse cannot make itself come alive, so it is impossible for unbelievers to rescue themselves from spiritual death.

3. List all the things in verses 4-10 that God did and has done for his people.
God has acted in great love and rich mercy towards his people (v 4); when we were spiritually dead, he made us alive in Christ (v 5); he raised us up with Christ (v 6); he has seated us in the heavenly realms, where he has seated Christ (v 6); he has given us the gift of faith, through which we can be saved by Christ (v 8); he has created us in Christ to do good works (v 10); he has prepared in advance the good works that he has saved us for (v 10).

- **What is the connection between Jesus**

Christ and the people that God saves through him? God's people receive these undeserved blessings and privileges by being united with Christ. Things that are true of Jesus (resurrection to eternal life, exaltation in heaven) are also true of all who are united to Jesus by faith, and they will be fully enjoyed by believers in the new creation.

4. What do these two lists together reveal about God's character? God's grace (his totally undeserved kindness) is literally "incomparable" (v 7). No one in any culture, in any part of history, in fact or in fiction has ever acted as God has here. The words "love", "mercy", "kindness" and "grace" only begin to describe how God has acted towards his people.

• **Looking at these verses, what characteristics will mark God's people in Christ?** The implications of these verses highlight signs that identify true believers, helping us to distinguish them from those who are only outwardly religious. True believers…
  • have a story of their life that divides into two: life before Christ and life united with Christ (v 1-3 vs. v 4-10).
  • freely confess their sin (v 1-3).
  • understand that they are not right with God because they are better people but because God has shown them incomparable grace (v 4-5, 8).
  • don't boast about being right with God because they know they have contributed nothing (v 9).
  • thank God for the gift of faith (v 8).
  • do good works because that is what they have been created in Christ to do (v 10).

5. What will be the effect of Christ's church in this world (v 7)? God's purpose is that through all the stories and changed lives of those in the church, the "incomparable riches of his grace" will be revealed and displayed to future generations of humanity, and perhaps on into eternity too (v 7).

• **What part do his people play to bring this about (v 10)?** This happens when people who were once dead in sins, disobedient, lustfully selfish and deserving only of God's wrath are saved by faith in Christ and go on to do good works, which, it turns out, God has planned for them.

EXPLORE MORE
How does this Old Testament prophecy [Isaiah 11:1-10] reflect some of the things that we have learned about the church of Christ so far (in this session or previous ones)?
• The Branch or Root of Jesse (Isaiah 11:1, 10), on whom the Spirit rests (v 2), who delights in the one true God (v 3), who judges with righteousness and rules with sovereign power (v 4) is revealed in the New Testament to be Jesus (Revelation 22:16)—the King of the kingdom that is the church.
• Creatures that on earth are never found together live side by side (Isaiah 11:8)—just as people from many and various people groups are unified by the lordship of Jesus Christ, seen most startlingly and wonderfully in the fellowship between Jewish and Gentile believers in the early church.
• The earth filled with the knowledge of God (v 9) depicts the outworking of God's plan for Christ's work in this world. Everyone will marvel at the incomparable riches of God's grace when they see and understand what the church of Christ is: helpless, hopeless sinners rescued by the mercy and kindness of God in Jesus Christ.

6. APPLY: "We are God's handiwork, created in Christ Jesus to do good works, which God prepared in advance for us to do." What does this look like in your church, and in your life? Get people to list some of the good works seen in your church. Include the widest range possible: from upfront responsibilities to behind-the-scenes activities; formal organised activities or informal reactive ones; in the church community or the local community; deeds and words; activities that encompass evangelism, gospel understanding, encouragement, practical help, training, motivating, sharing of burdens, resourcing gospel ministry, or accountability. For ideas, look at New Testament examples: e.g. Acts 9:36-39; 1 Timothy 5:10; 6:18; Titus 2:1-10; Hebrews 10:24-25. This question aims (1) to encourage Christians to see all the good things that happen and that wouldn't take place if your church didn't exist, and (2) to give ideas of good deeds to get involved with.

• **How do we make sure that it's God's incomparable grace that is displayed through our good deeds?** We need to proclaim the gospel alongside the good deeds that we do. Otherwise people will conclude that we are simply nice people. Titus 2 shows how good deeds support the proclamation of the gospel (v 5, 8, 10) and flow from the work of the gospel in people's lives (v 11-14).

7. Paul talks in these verses about a "mystery"—a big truth that God did not reveal to his people before the age of the apostles, but which Paul is now proclaiming to the church at Ephesus. What is it (v 6)? Through the gospel both Jews and Gentiles become one body, and both share together in all that was promised to Israel, which is now fulfilled in Jesus.

In the Old Testament the nation of Israel were God's chosen people; Gentiles could only be included by giving up any other national allegiance to join Israel. But Jesus' death and resurrection means that Gentiles can become part of God's people without needing to become Jewish first. Although this is often hinted at in the Old Testament, it was hidden from most Jewish people.

8. What, then, is unique about the message of the gospel and the church that it produces? The gospel has the power to unite people groups as disparate and mutually hostile as the Jews and Gentiles were, so that together they become one body under the headship of Jesus Christ. If the gospel can do this with Jews and Gentiles—divided by the most deep-rooted, long-lasting and intractable hostility imaginable—it can cross any human divide, whether national, ethnic, political or social. Crucially, beyond turning to Christ as Lord and submitting to the word of God, people don't need to change what they are to join the church—their nationality, ethnicity, class, culture, level of education and so on. This unity without uniformity is what makes the church unique.

9. What will be the effect of Christ's church on the entire cosmos (v 10-11)? Verse 10 tells us what God's plan has always been: that the church of Christ will showcase the multi-coloured wisdom of God to all spiritual rulers and authorities in the heavenly realms. John Piper explains how that works: "What the church is to do is demonstrate the wisdom in God's mysterious plan. The wisdom of a plan is seen by the fact that it works. We show the wisdom of God by showing in the church that it is working. The death of Christ was not in vain: it has reconciled us to God, it has broken down the wall of hostility between Jew and Gentile and other races, it has produced one new body, and it has given us the hope of his immeasurable kindness forever. We show the wisdom of God to the cosmic powers by living this way, by being the church Christ died to create." (desiringgod.org/messages/the-cosmic-church [March 22 1981], accessed 23/6/20)

10. APPLY: When is it hard to remember that the church is God's masterpiece to display his glory to the cosmos? So often our churches look weak and unimpressive, and increasingly pushed to the cultural margins. Sunday by Sunday, we're just an ordinary bunch of people gathering to do something that looks very insignificant in the eyes of most. Or perhaps we are discouraged by trials or it looks as if evil is "winning". But these verses encourage us: God is at work to display his wisdom to the world and beyond. That may not be seen fully now, but one day it will be.

• **At those times, how can we help one another to lift our eyes to what God is doing through his church?** Encourage your group to share ideas. Perhaps we need to be more intentional in giving thanks to God for our church—its very existence is an astonishing miracle!

11. APPLY: What excites you most about this idea of the church as God's masterpiece? In what ways is it better than the other "bigger stories" you talked about in question 1? The story of what God is doing in the world and the universe is one that will not end; it will not go out of date. It will not be undone by our own death, or by the fall of a leader. We need not be frustrated when progress is slow. God will finish what he has started. This story does not depend on us—it depends on him.

8 Acts 6:1-7; Acts 8 and 11
CHURCH IN THIS WORLD

THE BIG IDEA
Despite all that we've learned, our experience of church can be disappointing or difficult, and this was also the experience of the first church, which faced problematic relationships within and persecution from outside; yet God used all of this to grow and bless his people.

SUMMARY
In the previous seven sessions we have seen God's intimate love and cosmic purposes for the church of Christ, which brings believers unimaginable security and privileges as part of the church. Nevertheless, for all believers the day-to-day experience of life in a local church can often be difficult and disappointing. This was even true of the first church in Jerusalem.

Within a church, the thing most likely to blight our experience is relationship problems. In Acts chapter 6 a difficulty arose within the Jerusalem church between two distinct groups of Jewish believers: those who were Hellenistic (brought up under the influence of Greek language and culture) and those who were Hebraic (whose Jewishness was unaffected by Greek culture and language). It seems that the Hellenistic believers were not being treated on equal terms with Hebraic Jewish believers in respect of food distribution to widows.

Interestingly, the apostles didn't set up an investigation into what exactly had happened and why; rather they focused on enabling reconciliation and unity, by ensuring that food would be distributed fairly in the church. Their priority was to implement a practical solution that also

would not distract them from their own fundamental ministry of preaching the word and prayer. This episode gives us a glimpse of the importance of the body, where all parts are needed for the health of the whole church. The apostles could not have solved the relationship problem in the church by themselves; they needed the commitment and faithfulness of the men who were chosen to supervise the food distribution. There are many wise insights that can be gathered from the way the apostles went about dealing with the relationship problem in Jerusalem. The result of the apostles' solution was that the church grew rapidly.

From outside the church it was persecution that caused most difficulty for the first believers. The opposition of Saul of Tarsus to the church became more aggressive and was targeted against even ordinary believers after the martyrdom of Stephen. As a result, the church in Jerusalem was scattered across Judea and Samaria. In Acts chapters 8 and 11 we see that although the believers were forced to move, they continued to act as they had always done: faithfully preaching the word to the people they encountered in new areas. Again, the result of these difficulties was that the word of God spread, and new local churches sprang up in many different places.

These stories of the first church should help us to see that God is always in control and at work no matter how difficult the problems are that we face—whether they are caused by difficult relationships or bitter opposition. If we continue to be faithful in preaching and ministering the gospel, all these problems become opportunities for unbelievers to hear the good news and for the church to grow.

OPTIONAL EXTRA

Tell your favourite story of how something really good came out of a really bad situation: it might be a personal experience, or a true story from history, or a fictional one from a film or book. See if other people can share the same sort of story.

GUIDANCE FOR QUESTIONS

1. What kinds of things sometimes make our experience of church disappointing or difficult? The most likely answer is when relationships go sour. This is inevitable since in this world followers of Jesus still struggle with sin, and all of us need to mature in wisdom and godliness. As we will see, the first church struggled with difficult relationships among its members, and the apostles rightly recognised that the problem was serious. Another difficulty that we face is hostility and opposition from enemies of the gospel. Both difficulties can take away our joy in belonging to God's people.

2. What problem emerged in the first church in Jerusalem? Though all of the believers at this time were Jewish, they came from two distinct groups: the Hebraic Jews and the Hellenistic Jews (see dictionary, p 49). The Hellenistic Jews complained that their widows were not getting a fair share in the daily distribution of food to all believing widows in need. (See 1 Timothy 5:3-16 for a full description of this ministry in the early church.)

- **What caused this problem, do you think?** It's not clear why the Hebraic Jewish widows were prioritised when it came to the church's food distribution. This was not necessarily due to overt favouritism. It could have been an example

of unconscious ethnic bias: thoughtless behaviour towards people from a different ethnic group in which unfair treatment results from assumptions and stereotypes about that ethnic group. There is a well-known human tendency to notice, gravitate towards and get to know best those who are most like ourselves, with the consequence that we don't think of or even see those from different groups. However, both overt and unconscious favouritism are unacceptable in the church of Christ, which we know will eternally comprise believers of all tribes, tongues and nations. So, whatever the reason, urgent action was required to ensure that the testimony of the church would not be spoiled.

3. What dilemma did this problem present to the apostles? The apostles were resolute about the importance of prioritising the preaching of the word and prayer in their own ministries. They knew that personal involvement in food distribution would distract them from those priorities, and the church would suffer worse harm. But ignoring the problem was not an option.

- **How would ignoring the problem have affected the church's gospel ministry?** It would have undermined the cosmic testimony of the church to the wisdom of God (see Session 7), seen when Christ's people, drawn from all the tribes, languages and people groups of the earth, are united as one body in him. If not even two groups of Jewish people could live together harmoniously in the church, what hope could there be for that greater unity promised in the gospel?

4. What was so good about the solution the apostles came up with? It meant that the apostles could continue to focus on the ministries of prayer and preaching the word of God. But it also underlined how seriously they took this matter, as can be seen, first, by the fact that all twelve apostles jointly decided on a resolution and summoned all the disciples to hear the solution (v 2), and second, by the careful process by which they implemented the decision (v 3). They underlined the importance of the food-distribution ministry by specifying that those responsible for supervising it must be "full of the Spirit and wisdom". They then ensured that everyone would have confidence in those supervisors by giving the final choice to the church.

- **How does it illustrate the importance of the church acting as a body (see Session 5)?** The apostles could not have solved this problem by themselves. That would have meant neglecting the overriding priorities of preaching the word and prayer. They needed other faithful and committed believers to supervise the food distribution.

5. What snippets of godly wisdom for church life can we learn from this story?

Get people to think about: the apostles' priorities; what they didn't do that we might have expected them to do; the guidance they gave for choosing men for the new ministry; the process they set up for selecting those men; and their level of involvement in the new ministry.

- Not even important matters should distract leaders gifted in teaching and preaching from carrying out that foundational responsibility, along with the vital ministry of praying for the church (v 4).
- As far as we know, the leaders did not launch an investigation into why the Hebraic Jews were at fault. They focused on finding a solution. In the murky context

of difficult relationships, moving forward in a spirit of repentance, forgiveness, love and unity must be the priority rather than raking over past events in an effort to apportion blame. (*Note:* This doesn't mean that church leaders should never investigate and impose sanctions in the context of reported wrongdoing. The New Testament church leaders were unafraid to do this—see, for example, Acts 5:1-9; 1 Corinthians 5:1-5; Galatians 2:11-14; 2 Thessalonians 3:6, 14-15; Titus 1:10-13; 3 John:9-10.)

- No matter how mundane a church ministry seems, the most important quality to look for in someone to carry out that ministry must be evidence of the work of the Spirit in the person's character (v 3). Character trumps gifting.
- Leaders should not impose their choice of people on the church congregation. The people of the church need to have some part in choosing those who will serve among them (v 3). Otherwise, those given responsibilities might not have the confidence of the congregation and be unable to carry out their ministries effectively; and members could well feel unappreciated, leading to the danger of a full-blown division in the church. Leaders need the knowledge and insight of others to overcome any blind spots regarding the people they might prefer for a role.
- On the other hand, the church should not choose people to serve and run ministries without the approval and involvement of church leaders (v 6). Church members need the wisdom of their leaders and should understand that leaders often know things about people that are relevant to their suitability for a ministry but have to be kept confidential.
- Leaders should not micro-manage the church's ministries. Once people who are

acceptable to everyone have been chosen for a ministry, they should take day-to-day responsibility for that ministry (v 3b-4).

6. What was the effect of sorting out the church's problem, according to Luke (v 7)?

Luke follows the story of the problem in the church with a description of the church's growth. The word of God spread, and the number of disciples in Jerusalem increased rapidly. Perhaps most surprisingly, given that the Jewish religious establishment had produced the most hostile of Jesus' enemies, a large number of priests became believers. All of this, it seems, was the direct result of the church being equipped to preach and teach the gospel without distraction and to serve the needs of all believers in a way that displayed their miraculous unity in the Spirit.

7. APPLY: What divisions could occur in your church family?

All churches have groups and ministries that focus on a select group of people—children, youth, students, seniors, internationals and so on—either for evangelism or to teach and disciple more effectively and relevantly. Problems arise when believers can't relate to fellow Christians outside of their specific group, and a them-and-us attitude develops. The beauty and miracle of Christ's church is that the Spirit binds into one unity many people of great diversity. As church members, we should be able to count as brothers and sisters those who are ethnically different from us, older or younger than us, from different socio-economic backgrounds, perhaps with a different first language to ours, and in different stages of life as regards singleness, marriage, parenthood, bereavement, education, and work or retirement. Useful questions to ask the group include: Are there groups in your

church from which you don't know anyone or with whom you feel you have very little in common? Do you have good relationships with believers who are significantly different to you in some way? How diverse are those in church to whom you are close?

- **How could you help the leaders in your church to overcome these sorts of problems?**
  - Pray for unity—it's the work of the Spirit to help us understand the gospel such that we are bound together in unity with all believers.
  - Take the initiative in bridging gaps between people or groups in your church—warm, Christian friendships are the antidote to the stereotyping and misunderstandings that cause unconscious bias and strained relationships between people of different groups.
  - Listen to your leaders and act on their Bible teaching. Godly, faithful church leaders will make church unity a priority because the New Testament makes it a priority.

8. What were the means by which the church grew?

Acts 8:1: God used persecution to make the believers scatter throughout Judea and Samaria, as they moved away from Jerusalem to escape the actions of Saul, who was determined and able to imprison every believer he could find. *Verse 4:* The scattered believers "preached the word wherever they went". Although they wanted to escape Saul's persecution, they were not so intimidated by it that they stopped witnessing about Jesus. *Acts 11:19-20:* Some of the scattered believers focused on preaching the gospel to ethnically and culturally Jewish people— the people of Christ and his apostles—but others reached out to the separate cultural group of Greek-speaking Jewish people. Vitally, the Lord's hand was with all these believers as they evangelised (v 21).

9. What were the means by which the new church at Antioch was established?
Verse 22: The church in Jerusalem sent Barnabas. This was probably for three reasons: (1) to check that what was happening at Antioch truly was the same work of the Spirit through the same gospel that had taken place in Jerusalem; (2) so that the new church in Antioch could be encouraged and helped by people from the older church, like Barnabas, with greater experience of Christian life and ministry; and (3) to establish a connection between the two churches demonstrating that both groups were part of the one body of Christ. *Verses 25-26:* Barnabas and Saul devoted a whole year to teaching these new believers. This shows the importance not just of seeing people turn to faith in Christ but of making disciples, by teaching new believers from God's word all that they need to know to follow Jesus and serve others faithfully and enduringly come what may.

10. After these events, how might faithful believers have viewed persecution, do you think?
Their experience of persecution must have been traumatic for those first believers, suddenly forcing them to flee from their homes and perhaps abandon their livelihoods, friends and family, and security. However, after some time, both they and those who had received the gospel from the migrants would have been able to look back and see how God had used persecution to grow the church in many other places outside of Jerusalem. They would have learned a dramatic lesson about God's sovereignty and how, despite all human opposition,

his purposes always prevail. They would be helped to trust him in all circumstances.

11. APPLY: What persecution could your church face? How might God use that, do you think?
In the West today, persecution is most likely to occur when unbelievers, especially those with atheistic, secular humanist beliefs, encounter the Bible-based beliefs of your church or church members that are now deeply countercultural—beliefs on issues such as abortion and euthanasia, sex education, gay and transgender rights, and the role of women; and activities such as outreach to those of other faiths, street evangelism, and even expressing a personal opinion in a private conversation or message in some contexts. Persecution can involve social-media harassment, public criticism, withdrawal of permission to use premises for Christian meetings, public protests or campaigns orchestrated against churches or individuals, disciplinary procedures at work or dismissal from employment, calling on the police to stop a Christian activity, and legal action.

Talk about which of these or other issues are most likely to cause difficulties for your church or people in your group. Make sure you don't just talk about the difficulties but also the opportunities.

• **How can you help fellow believers to remain true to the Lord when your church faces hostility and opposition?**
  • New or untaught believers need to know that persecution is the normal experience of the church of Christ worldwide and in history. See Jesus' words in John 15:20. Persecution for the gospel doesn't mean that believers have done wrong in God's sight.
  • They also need to know that God is sovereign over all circumstances—even

those that are painful for believers. Take them to Bible passages like Acts 8 and 11 to show them how God has done great things for his church through persecution in the past.

- Encourage others by your example, especially in refusing to be ashamed of churches or Christians who face persecution for the gospel, and in continuing to speak and act faithfully as a disciple of Jesus despite opposition.
- Get people to share any other ideas or insights that they may have.

12. APPLY: What have you learned, in this session and all of these studies, that will help you to stick with your brothers and sisters in Christ and remain true to the Lord with all your heart? Give people some time to look back through this booklet and think through the things they have learned about the church that have had the greatest impact on them. Encourage people to share how those truths help them to persevere and to prioritise Christ's church throughout life.

Good Book Guides
The full range

thegoodbook

COMPANY

BIBLICAL | RELEVANT | ACCESSIBLE

At The Good Book Company, we are dedicated to helping Christians and local churches grow. We believe that God's growth process always starts with hearing clearly what he has said to us through his timeless word—the Bible.

Ever since we opened our doors in 1991, we have been striving to produce Bible-based resources that bring glory to God. We have grown to become an international provider of user-friendly resources to the Christian community, with believers of all backgrounds and denominations using our books, Bible studies, devotionals, evangelistic resources, and DVD-based courses.

We want to equip ordinary Christians to live for Christ day by day, and churches to grow in their knowledge of God, their love for one another, and the effectiveness of their outreach.

Call us for a discussion of your needs or visit one of our local websites for more information on the resources and services we provide.

Your friends at The Good Book Company

01224 681540